THE DRUG EPIDEMIC

What It Means and How
To Combat It

THE DRUG EPIDEMIC

What It Means and How To Combat It

by Dr. Wesley C. Westman

: THE DIAL PRESS : *New York*

Library of Congress Catalog Card Number 70-102832 : Printed in the United States of America : Typography by Jane Byers Bierhorst : First Printing

To my parents, Violet and Meade L. Westman,
my wife, Noelene Raiford Westman,
and my children, Mark and Charlene

AUTHOR'S PREFACE

Drugs have become a central issue of our time. They separate young from old, revolutionary from reactionary, and parent from child. The addict of ten years ago was from the ghetto; he picked up his habit in the streets. Written off as a loss to society for many reasons other than drugs, he was seen as a criminal and treated as one. The junkie of today is in even more trouble. And there is a new addict in addition to the ghetto addict, the product of a society changing too rapidly. His parents are caught in the traps of economic squeeze and family breakdown, which have come on the heels of the downfall of many of our traditional American values. Marriage and the family, achievement and technology, and a dehumanized and plastic world feed the pathology of a society that has produced a nation of junkies.

In looking at this problem, we will see ourselves on most of the pages in this book: what we had and what we seem to have lost, the sense of family and community that keeps us feeling alive and involved. We seem to be suffering from feelings of being powerless, helpless, useless, and very often hopeless. Too many have sold so much in return for so little that our collective rush to synthetic experience is no surprise. But it is therefore even more tragic. We may be hooked on food, work, alcohol, or drugs, but it seems that many of us have some type of habit to kick. In the process we may come back to a state of existence that truly deserves the word "community."

The observations and descriptions found in this book are the result of my more than three years of involvement with drug-addiction programs and drug addicts. My work took place at first in the streets, then in the New York State program, and subsequently in the Connecticut State program and in my private office. It is the result of my own style of involvement with people while attempting to extract meaning from these experiences. After a time certain patterns began to emerge which stood out in bolder relief than the less consistent kinds of patterns.

This book describes groups of people that have been addicted to drugs, in most cases heroin. The descriptions in most of the chapters come from the concentrated experiences of marathon groups in Beacon, New York, where former addicts became residents of a new center for rehabilitation when that center first opened. That institution's residents were largely from the New York City area. Subsequent work in Connecticut has helped me with the revisions I have made since first writing the text.

Most of the material in this book is about the new addict, not the ghetto addict. The new addict seems to have much more of the personal, family, and peer-group disturbance that leads to addiction. If you were to stay in a ghetto area for any length of time, you would probably wonder why there are so few addicts, not why there are so many. But the higher-income residential neighborhoods do not show why addiction occurs there. The people who have lived there do say how it happens, and this even sheds some light on which people from the ghetto choose drugs rather than some other form of disorder.

Observations that seem to hold true about the broad problem of drug addiction in all the various settings are:

1 : Drug addiction, like other human behavior, has no *single* cause.

2 : Addiction is interwoven with the entire fabric of human problems now existing in our society.

3 : No single group of individuals will ever be able to curb the growth of addiction, let alone eliminate it.

4 : Progress in working with the problem of drug addiction will be effective only if a comprehensive approach is used.

5 : The success of efforts to end drug abuse will depend upon the degree to which related social problems are simultaneously attacked.

Observations about drug abusers that hold true are:

1 : The first drug experience evidently either produces specific good feelings or perceptions, or eliminates unwanted feelings or perceptions, or both.
2 : Drug abusers spend much time, money, and trouble in trying to recapture the essence of that first experience, which is quite clearly not possible.
3 : All illicit drugs are deceptive, and their proponents promise much more than the drugs can deliver.
4 : The changes in states of feeling and altered levels of consciousness can be achieved by methods not involving the use of drugs, if that is really the goal involved.

One last thought. To the addicts: There are those who give a damn. If you get out, there are those who will care enough to help you stay out. Then you can help others out. And maybe then you can help people with other problems too. I do it for a living, and I like it. I think you will too, because we are alike in many ways. . . .

CONTENTS

THE DRUG EPIDEMIC

What It Means and How
To Combat It

1 : THE ADDICTION-PRONE PERSON

There are as many reasons to try drugs as there are drugs. A willingness to try anything once is almost a part of our national character. But there are obvious differences between the people who try drugs and the people who continue to use them. The users are people who share a set of personal characteristics. They are petulant and manipulative, immature and perpetually unhappy people. They have very little control over their impulses and seem unable to gain satisfaction from the things that give most people pleasure. For these individuals, the permanently disenchanted, pleasure comes in a bag or a capsule or a pill.

The addiction-prone person probably came from a family where an extremely serious imbalance of power existed. The same-sex parent may have been either extremely submissive or extremely domineering. This situation is treated in some detail in Chapter 8, "Family Influences." At any rate the child usually perceives a wide discrepancy of power between his parents. Sensing this wide discrepancy, the child may develop very early a deep sense of injustice and a hatred for authoritarian people and authority figures in general; e.g., teachers, principals, and policemen. The child may also feel that he himself is powerless in a power-oriented environment, that he must always be on guard, and that he must resort to verbal manipulation of others to gain what he wants.

Since deep and meaningful love is usually not possible in such a setting, what the child wants are usually things—objects that are rewards to make up for lost love. The victimized parent very often is more than willing to buy "things" in order to get the little attention and affection the child will give in return. It is not likely that the child in such a family will choose to emulate either the brute or the jellyfish, and whatever religious or moral values the parents do profess will also be rejected on the basis of the difference between what they say and what they do.

Thus the basis for the addiction-prone personality is valuing things more than people, an early tendency to manipulate others verbally for selfish ends, and the absence of an ego ideal and conscience. The school years are likely to reinforce and strengthen this pattern if the child can maintain his status as a successful operator, or they will reinforce it negatively if the student is identified as a behavior problem and can enjoy the secret admiration of his peers.

Influence of friends becomes more and more important as one approaches puberty. If the individual with a behavior problem in school has a model-student brother or sister to whom he is constantly and unfavorably compared, the gang will become a substitute family with whom he can enjoy some kind of recognition and status. The incidence of street gangs vs. clubs may be dependent, in part, upon differences in geography and socioeconomic status, but these differences are rapidly disappearing. Even the richest suburban schools now have both formal and informal gangs in which antiauthoritarian and, by extension, antisocial activities are part of the accepted mores.

For such groups that which is forbidden is attractive. If school authorities make rules against smoking and drinking, they are presenting a dare. It would then be inconsistent for the group to do anything but begin to smoke and drink, whether they really liked it or not. Breaking the rules becomes normal behavior for such gangs. That which is defined as wrong by authorities usually becomes a challenge to live up to, a set of behaviors they seem obliged to perpetuate.

Many high-school dropouts turn to more serious attempts to get even with "the brute," who by now has been extended beyond the original parent to include anyone who makes or enforces rules. If drugs are available, they use and usually abuse them. Or they may smoke or drink alcohol, or simply show passive–aggressive nonparticipation in what is expected by parents or teachers. It should be made explicit at this point that the addiction-prone person may or may not become addicted to, or misuse, one kind of drug or another. The lives of those who escape actual drug use may be marked by chronic malaise and anxiety, shallow interpersonal relationships, a lack of goal orientation, and permanent petulant dissatisfaction, although they may have some vocational success.

Such people are usually bright and, at times, creative. Their sexual adjustment is usually marginal and lacks deeper meaning: that is, it represents seduction success and a method of reducing tension rather than an expression of love. Sexual identity is usually very shaky; active or passive participation in homosexual activities in time of need is common, especially in institutional settings. Such people have very little control over their impulses. If they do control impulses, it is at the expense of others; i.e., there must be something explicit in it for them. They are the permanently disenchanted. One of the myths about drugs is that they induce or increase sexual appetites. The opposite is more often true. The bravado of chicks and broads and dudes and studs is usually a sign of deeply ingrained sexual confusion. Concerns about sexual adequacy and power issues in love and sex all take time and effort to work through. Most drug users prefer to avoid this hassle and seek their release through drugs.

It should also be made explicit that drug users come from every ethnic group and socioeconomic status. Negro, Puerto Rican, and Mexican Americans show up more than others in statistical tables of "scientific" surveys and in institutions for drug addicts. But people from lower socioeconomic levels generally get caught more frequently in all categories of lawbreaking, so these statistics are not really valid. Furthermore, the number of people dependent on drugs who are able to hide their problem increases as one proceeds up the socioeconomic ladder. The impression that drug abuse is limited mainly to lower-income groups is one of the many social myths we maintain in order to explain the phenomenon of drug addiction and to justify prison sentences for drug offenders.

It is apparent that as a nation we learned little from the days of Prohibition. Making any substance illegal simply creates a lively black-market delivery system; in effect, the laws make drugs more expensive and of questionable strength and purity. Until we are willing to treat the *causes* rather than the *effects* of drug abuse, drug addiction will continue to be a serious problem. In an economic sense, a good treatment program would cost each state about one-tenth the amount of money it takes, in stolen goods and property, to support drug habits. Some police officials have estimated that in areas with a high concentration of addicts in the United States between fifty and seventy-five percent of all crimes are related directly or indirectly to drug abuse.

The addict who is "strung out," or unable to get high with any amount of heroin, will purchase drugs on the street in broad daylight, hoping a cop is watching. He doesn't even want to make the decision to seek detoxification, even when he knows he wants it. He hopes that the narcotics-squad detective who is watching will make it for him. If he is arrested, or "busted," he can always claim to his friends that it was just bad luck and that he didn't "chump himself" by volunteering for treatment or a rehabilitation program. It's called the drug scene.

The drug-addicted person is often extremely sensitive and vulnerable. The time he spends high on drugs is wasted. Having missed all the toughening developmental tasks of establishing an identity separate from the family, preparing for and entering an appropriate and mature heterosexual relationship, receiving the growth in self-esteem possible from work done well, and many other normal experiences, he feels inadequate to any task except continuing to "chase the bag" of heroin in the streets. He is caught up in a never-ending cycle of prison, state mental hospitals, and the path leading back to the "cooker," where those little white crystals, heated with water and injected into the bloodstream, will carry him away from it all, if only for a few hours.

When drug-free, or in an institution, these people can be interesting, kind, and considerate. They can also be bitter and hostile, striking out at authority figures and at any form of pretense in the professional who is attempting to help them. They are probably the most interesting, challenging, and frustrating of all people to work with.

Although psychodynamics will be discussed in more detail in a later chapter, it should be stated at this point that drug addiction is often mistakenly thrown into several popular categories, such as those of psychopathic or sociopathic personalities. But although addicts seem to be dumped into the category of character disorders, my experience is that careful diagnosis would indicate a wider range of psychic disorders.

If one had to estimate the number of addiction-prone people as compared to the number of those actually addicted to alcohol or other drugs, it would have to be strictly a guess, but my guess would be that of those people under the age of twenty-five in the United States, there are probably fifty addiction-prone persons for every addict. Similarly the number of known addicts as compared to the actual number must also be a guess. But if you take the number of known addicts and multiply it by four or five, you will probably have a rough estimate of the actual number in any geographic area.

A historical perspective must also be added. Before 1914 a large number of people in the United States were addicted to patent medicines. People with arthritis and other illnesses could buy these medicines without prescription at their corner drugstore. So when we speak of the addiction-prone person and the addict, we are speaking of the present time, present laws, and present social conditions in the United States.

Although there are similarities among drug abusers, their individual differences in the choice of drugs vary according to their personal experiences. And those who start and stay with marijuana differ markedly from those who use "acid" (LSD), and both differ from the alcoholic or the heroin addict. Barbiturate addicts are something else again, and the "speed freak," on Methedrine or some other amphetamine, is thought weird even by other addicts.

Unless otherwise specified in context, when the word

"addict" is used in this book, it refers to an individual who has had a mainline habit of some duration with heroin or some other opiate. This is because the bulk of my experience has been with such addicts and because, in terms of numbers, they are the largest group in the country who most need treatment and rehabilitation and who receive it least.

This picture is changing slowly, with state programs in operation in New York and California and a new federal law (the Narcotics Addiction Rehabilitation Act of 1966). This new law provides for treatment in federal facilities and for follow-up services to be provided in the addict's hometown. But all programs are underfinanced, understaffed, and tremendously overburdened. For every one hundred addicts rehabilitated during any given year, there may be five hundred who have begun new habits.

2 : THE DRUGS

The poppy, like the man said, is also a flower. In *The Wizard of Oz,* before Dorothy and her traveling companions reached the Emerald City, the Wicked Witch of the West arranged for their trip to take them through a field of poppies. Even Frank Baum knew about the narcotic effects in the pods of some poppies. *Papaver somniferum* is the Latin designation for this kind of poppy, a small innocuous little flower that kills people. It is not a man-eating plant, but when the sticky substance in the pod is refined into morphine, subsequently refined into heroin, shipped to the consumer, and injected into the vein of a human being, the black sleep promised by the designation of the substance (narcotic) turns out, very often, to be permanent. A lot of people die from it every day. The drug scene is not hip. The mystique surrounding drugs attracts young people. The designation "forbidden fruit" given by legislative bodies acting upon the advice of blue-ribbon panels of physicians and health officials has had little effect on drug abuse.

Since the time that drugs and alcohol have been restricted legally, there has been a continuous battle over whose domain is involved. Penologists and physicians have been saddled at various times with the primary responsibility. At times they have sought this major responsibility, and at times they have avoided it. Current legislation defining drug addiction and alcoholism as diseases would indicate the extension of medical prerogatives into these areas. But who has primary statute responsibility seems to have little effect on the actual practice of the addict or alcoholic.

Most addicts are caught up in a very real version of the game cops and robbers, which is learned in the streets and taught in most penal institutions. It is a deadly serious game, but a game nonetheless. It involves rules on both sides. The same family may produce an older son who becomes a cop and a younger son who becomes a robber.

Back to the drugs—the substances used and misused by millions of people. To cover the entire range in depth would be an encyclopedic undertaking, but drug groups can be mentioned, along with some of their street names. But before launching this task, we must be honest about drugs. Most of us use them, and many of us misuse them. The ones we use happen to be legal; for example, caffeine, nicotine, and even the tannic acid in tea. We take diet pills which contain amphetamines and sleeping pills when they are prescribed by a physician. Tons of tranquilizers are taken by Americans to take the edge off the anxiety of surviving in the economic jungle. We are in the middle of a drug revolution, and it is by no means bloodless.

The addict who mainlines heroin and who fears the "O.D." (death due to overdose) lets blood seep into the syringe slowly, then very carefully shoots in a little of the blood-drug mixture called "gravy." He waits for this to take effect and, based upon his feeling, or "high," he may then shoot some more gravy . . . through a dirty needle . . . with junk that has probably been cut three or four times with milk sugar . . . in a stinking room with cockroaches and a squeaky bed . . . always fearing the too heavy load which leads to that permanent black sleep.

A kid in San Francisco is lying on the sidewalk. He jumped fifteen stories as a result of the effects of LSD. He thought he could fly. He wanted to be free, to be a bird. His blood trickles down the sidewalk, into the gutter, through the sewer system, and maybe out into the blue Pacific. Free at last!

It is not bloodless, and it is a revolution, or a rapid and remarkable change. In the days before psychiatric drugs received wide acceptance (in the early 1950's), severely mentally ill patients had no hope of adequate treatment. The treatments were worse than the sickness:

insulin shock, electroshock, and even psychosurgery, during which the frontal lobes of the brains of unmanageable patients were quickly disconnected. It made people into zombies. Current drug therapy enables many formerly "hopeless" chronic schizophrenics to return to family, home, and even work. So drugs also can save lives and relieve suffering.

"The fault, dear Brutus, is . . . in ourselves" for believing in instant happiness, instant success, instant relief. Drugs are drugs, and like the hatchet, they can hew a house from a tree or split the skull of a man, depending on who is using them and for what.

The impatience of the disenchanted is such that time is of the essence. Feelings are rulers that have little patience. We feel that we should be able to be happy, free of anxiety, well-liked by others, talented, and successful. And we magically believe that since we *feel* that way, it should *be* that way. When this doesn't happen, we feel justified in rearranging our internal world by using drugs, since the uncooperative outer world has not yet rearranged itself to our satisfaction.

The drug families include narcotics, psychic energizers such as amphetamines, barbiturates, tranquilizers, and hallucinogens such as LSD. Marijuana and related cannabislike drugs are often legally grouped with narcotics, but they are actually mild hallucinogens. A brief description of each drug family follows:

Narcotics : Most narcotic drugs (other than synthetic narcotics) are derivatives of the *Papaver somniferum* plant, the opium poppy. Morphine is the first derivative, heroin the second. Other drugs, like methadone, have similar effects, but heroin is the strongest illegal narcotic on the black market. It is called "stuff," "snow," "junk," "H," "horse," and "dope," among other things. Morphine is still used medically, but its use has dwindled, because nonaddicting pain relievers are now being produced in the laboratory. This has eliminated most of the legal need for the narcotics derived from this plant. The number and kind of synthetic narcotic substitutes is increasing. This allows physicians to withdraw heroin addicts from their habits by substituting one of these drugs for heroin and slowly reducing the dosage. Experimental programs use these drugs to maintain addicts for an indefinite period of time, during which other services, such as psychotherapy, are offered.

Psychic Energizers : These drugs are called "up" drugs or "uppers." They are the amphetamines—they lift mood, heighten sensory acuity, speed up speech and thought processes, and are diuretic. Taken over a long period of time, they may cause hallucinations, extreme suspiciousness, and even temporary toxic psychosis. Methedrine, or "speed," is the strongest, and the drug depression following an excessive dose of this drug can kill an individual. Speed comes in several forms: Benzedrine, or "bennies," Dexedrine, and many others. An older, related drug is cocaine, or "coke," which is often sniffed, or "snorted." It lifts the mood of the user. Cocaine is used far less today than previously. Amphetamines are often misused by students during examination periods. They are available at most truck stops for truck drivers on long hauls. They are also misused by the gamut of drug abusers who "need a lift." The high is often very pleasant, but coming down can result in deep depression. It would seem to be the psychic equivalent of Newton's third law of motion—for every (drug) action, there is an equal and opposite reaction.

Barbiturates : These are the "down" drugs. Seconal, Tuinal, Nembutal (the "redbirds," "bluebirds," and "yellow birds"), the "goofballs." A barbiturate addict is in trouble if he buys too many. He pops a few into his mouth and at first sinks pleasantly into oblivion. But he may lose track of how many he has popped and pop some more and then some more, and then he may die. These drugs are especially dangerous when mixed with alcohol.

Tranquilizers : The use of meprobamate and related drugs has increased very rapidly. These drugs are widely used, but as a general rule they are not widely misused, in that their effect is to relieve anxiety, a rather specific "bad" feeling. Few tranquilizers produce a specific new kind of feeling in normal doses; they don't pick you up, slow you down, or expand your mind to any noticeable degree. More than anything else, they simply enable you to function with less anxiety. However, continued excessive use may produce unwanted side effects.

Hallucinogens : These drugs have been called many things. Initially hallucinogens cause one to see, taste, and feel things that are not really there but that appear with all the frightening sharpness of synthetic reality. Under "normal" dosage (10 to 30 micrograms for an adult), sensations and perceptions begin to change their quality after a while and become more intense. Colors blur and fuse, and solid shapes sometimes become plastic. Fixation on one object may bring on intense experiences about the essential nature of things, and reports include insights into oneself and insights about the essential unity and interrelatedness of things. This is a good trip. A bad trip is a combination of a pyschotic episode (hence the term *psychotomimetic*), in which the effects of a psychosis or insanity are mimicked, and a nightmare over which one has no control. The most recent term is psychedelic, or mind-manifesting, the inference being that LSD allows an individual to see more of his conscious mind than he would under drug-free conditions. The assumption implicit in this term is that our experience with LSD will not add new dimensions or abilities to our minds but will instead reveal what is already there.

Most reports of experiences written both by expert and amateur users of the drug indicate that at the beginning of the trip LSD and other hallucinogens heighten awareness and aesthetic appreciation of perception and sensations, but that the dangerous part occurs when the trip begins to turn inward and repressed material from a life-experience begins to break into conscious awareness. A relatively strong individual who has a great deal of self-awareness before the trip may gain insight from this, but most often people who take LSD are not that kind of people, and their search for instant happiness ends at times in a mental hospital. However, in several studies made under carefully controlled conditions, LSD has been found to be a useful adjunct to psychotherapy. These conditions include proper dosage of the drug, selection of the patient, and continuous supervision during the experience, as well as, in some cases, the presence of a psychotherapist who has developed good rapport with the patient. A documentary film depicted the use of LSD as an adjunct to psychotherapy with alcoholic patients after an initial amount of rapport had been developed with a psychotherapist. Some significant gains were reported.

Unfortunately the panic that has made LSD illegal has also made it extremely difficult to continue valid research. There now seems to be a flurry of research aimed directly at documenting the damage done by LSD. Retinal damage and permanent chromosomal aberrations have been reported, along with brain damage and other negative effects. It would seem that neither the "positive" nor the "negative" evidence has been systematic, nor has it been convincing in terms of substantive conclusions.

There are still valid medical uses for most of these drugs, but this book deals only with abuses and abusers. The appropriate use of drugs is in the realm of medicine. Nobody really knows under what realm the drug abuser falls. This is a big part of the problem. Is it a medical problem, a mental-health problem, a penal problem, a social problem, or a psychological problem? It is all of these, and more—a political problem, a cultural-anthropological problem, a racial and ethnic problem; but most of all, it is a national problem of frightening proportions. We are truly experiencing a drug epidemic.

3 : THE BLACK MARKET

Just as a free-enterprise criminal system flourished as the result of Prohibition by trafficking in illegal alcohol, the same Mafia, or Cosa Nostra, began the establishment of illegal drug traffic, largely heroin, after World War II. In recent times those high up in the organization have felt that drug traffic is too risky, and they have backed away from it to some extent. The result in New York City is that two ethnic groups have taken up the wholesale and import functions, and many of those who bring in drugs are lone operators and amateurs, such as merchant seamen and airline employees. Since the drug traffic has passed into the hands of less-organized individuals, much greater danger is involved.

The first danger is the street pusher who sells so openly that he is likely to get both himself and the user arrested. These are dangers from the viewpoint of the addict. The second danger is that the user is never sure how strong the drug is, and at times he may get only garbage; that is, anything from milk sugar to baking soda with no heroin at all. Variations in concentration can lead to accidental overdose.

A "bag" of heroin presently sells for about three dollars. True market value would vary from only a few cents to a quarter if the drug were produced and sold legally. It was probably grown in a field somewhere in the Near or Middle East. A kilo (about 2.2 pounds) of raw opium, which is dark brown, dry, and brittle, may bring the farmer something like three hundred and fifty dollars, and by the time it gets to the streets of New York, it will be worth nearly a million dollars.

The chemical process for changing opium to morphine and subsequently into heroin is two chemical operations of different degrees of complexity—the first may be performed in a Mediterranean port city, the second, perhaps in France. For drugs from Mexican and South American sources, locations for these operations seem to be confined to the areas in the United States which are near Mexico.

After a wholesaler has received a bulk shipment, it has to be bagged, and it is usually cut first. At the present time anywhere from thirty to sixty-four bags comprise a load, depending on the size of the bags. Loads and half loads are dealers' quantities. Dealers may be wholesalers who sell to street pushers, retailers who sell on the streets, or addict pushers (with a "dealer's habit,") who have enough capital to buy large quantities, supply their own large habit and, after having sold what remains, have enough capital left to purchase another large quantity.

The myth of the pusher as an evil-eyed monster preying on young people and enticing them into lives of drug addiction doesn't hold up at present based on what addicts and exaddicts report. Most people either buy their own first bag or are given their first shot by an addict, who is usually a friend. The first experience with drugs for most hard-core addicts is with heroin. Most of them do not graduate to heroin from marijuana or other drugs. Their first experience was probably "skin popping" or "joy popping" (injecting under the skin but not directly into the vein). This takes a little longer to get an effect, the high is not so extreme, and the effect wears off more quickly.

Every addict who began skin popping with a weekend habit kept telling himself that he could control it —he would never get hooked. But most of them end up hooked and finally "strung out" so that no amount of heroin will really keep them as high as they want to be. They have to steal more and more, hustle and chase that bag, never knowing when the next one will come. Maybe the cops (narcotics-squad detectives) will move in and arrest the pushers and dealers they know. These panics send addicts looking for substitute drugs, such as Dolophine, Demerol, Dilaudid, codeine cough medicines, or paregoric.

A panic may also send them to private physicians, psychiatrists, mental hospitals, or to other rehabilitation programs. Addicts seldom seek professional help unless they want to bring their habits down to where smaller doses will again give them a high, or charges are pending, or family members force them into it.

Those who deal in drugs without being users are vultures who ply their trade with skill and cunning. They are so sly that law enforcement problems are enormous.

Importing

The Federal Bureau of Investigation, the Treasury Department, the Coast Guard, and the state and city police departments are all involved in attempting to halt the drug traffic, and they are very aware of the odds against success. The border guards at Tijuana have collected marijuana and other drugs literally by the ton. The United States shares approximately five thousand land miles of border with her neighbors to the north and south and has about four thousand miles of coastline. It would take every man in uniform today, in all the armed forces, even to begin to stop the inflow of drugs, at great inconvenience to ordinary travelers. It would take another force of equal size to inspect every ship, train, airplane, and other vehicle entering the United States each day, and this would nearly cripple ordinary commerce. One recent ingenious method used to smuggle heroin in pure form in from Mexico involved a man who took several young women to Mexico with him for a short "tourist visit." While they were there, they each swallowed several long balloons filled with heroin. They again crossed the border and reentered the United States with the heroin safely hidden in their stomachs; then they either regurgitated or excreted their balloons. Apparently they were not aware that if gastric juices or an accident had broken a balloon, they would have been dead in a matter of hours. This incident emphasizes the complexity of the enforcement problem with regard to drug importation.

It has been charged that the traffic in drugs very often takes place with the connivance of enforcement agents and police who are being paid off. In some cities, with some policemen, this may be true; but it is not the most important consideration. In most cities the narcotics squad is understaffed and overworked, and even if *every* enforcement agent were honest, the flow could not be stopped under these conditions.

Buying and Selling

The retail trade in illegal drugs is a likely business, with, at times, a one thousand percent profit from wholesale lots to bags on the street; and it obviously adds little to the Gross National Product. It may subtract several billion dollars a year from it, plus an inestimable cost in human lives and suffering. Add to that the cost of goods stolen to support habits and the rise in crime rates across the country.

It is not really possible to estimate precisely either the human cost or the economic loss. But consider an addict with an expensive habit, one hundred dollars a day. With a habit this heavy the addict obviously can't work. To obtain the hundred dollars in cash, he will probably have to obtain five hundred dollars worth of stolen goods (since a "fence" is seldom a charitable individual). Or he will have to mug, snatch purses, hit liquor stores or gas stations, and so forth, until he has enough funds to buy the drugs. The traffic in illegal drugs currently has a stranglehold on our common future.

The situation is obviously serious. For every pusher arrested, there seem to be two or three waiting; for every addict receiving rehabilitation services, there are four or five new addicts entering the drug scene. The obvious need is for broad, comprehensive programs that are closely tied to existing human-services programs. If this need is ignored, the consequences and complications will multiply gravely.

4 : PSYCHODYNAMICS

The addict's symptoms develop simultaneously with his habit, and those symptoms become superimposed upon the addiction-prone personality as described in general in Chapter 1. To some extent both the behavior pattern of the addiction-prone person and the personality of the active addict may be superimposed upon a deeper level of personality functioning which can either be basically pathological or relatively normal in the statistical sense of the word. As with everyone there are obvious levels, or layers, of personality, from the visible facade to the core of the individual.

The superficial level of functioning is most often diagnosed since it is descriptive of known behavior, and the diagnosis can therefore be defended on that basis. At this level of analysis all addicts could be diagnosed as showing character disorders, such as psychopathic, sociopathic, or antisocial, asocial, or dissocial reactions. To say an addict who steals to support his habit is antisocial may either be redundant or irrelevant, depending upon the individual. The basic motivation for the theft may be generally antisocial (the one who hates everybody), specifically antisocial (he doesn't like white businessmen in black neighborhoods), or simply a need to steal in order for him to support a habit which has grown beyond his ability to support by working. In the latter case the addict may not be anti-anybody; he simply hopes he won't get caught.

The symptoms of limited impulse control, lack of superego, distrust or fear of authority figures, manipulativeness, and hostility were there before the individual became an addict. The original pattern of personality functioning is strained or changed by the entire range of addiction-related behaviors and thus can add a second and distinct set of problems to the original problems.

It can be said of most addicts that they have very little self-esteem, show poorly developed egos, and have very little ego strength. An addict also tends to be extremely vulnerable, since staying high does not allow him to develop ego defenses to protect him from other people.

The "Straight" Addict

There are housewives, physicians, nurses, pharmacists, and a range of others who keep a small habit, support it through their own income, and generally avoid trouble with the law. They may occasionally volunteer for treatment, but it usually turns out to be because of guilt rather than because they are physiologically addicted. With a small habit one bag a day taken morning and evening will keep an individual straight and control most of his feelings and fears. A "bag" is a small glassine envelope which contains perhaps an ounce of white powder, most often with an unknown concentration of heroin. The rest of the mixture is either milk sugar, quinine, baking soda, or some other additive used to "cut" the heroin. What most straight addicts don't know is that if they stopped shooting heroin today, they would not likely suffer from any actual withdrawal symptoms other than those they induced themselves. Apparently they also don't know that with a doctor's prescription legal drugs are available that would probably control their specific "bad" feeling, whether anxiety, depression, or impending psychosis, much more effectively, more cheaply, and with no danger of arrest.

Individuals who need psychiatric care but can't afford it will usually be able to find clinical or other facilities either at a city, state, or federal agency or at a private agency. It may take effort, but the search is generally worth it. Mental-health services are usually listed in the telephone directory under city or state government.

There are addicts who use heroin without ever getting hooked. But they are the minority of heroin users who have more control over impulses and emotions and who use the drug as a middle-class neurotic might use tranquilizers, for personal relief from anxiety. Such people also use heroin so they will be more relaxed in social situations and more able to function on the job. It must be emphasized that these users are a very small group, for most "tasters" end up hooked.

The Hustler

This type of addict was probably addicted quite young, has few vocational skills that could support a habit, or simply has an aversion for work and doesn't have the stomach required to be a dealer or a pusher, or the proclivities to be a pimp. He runs con games in the street, in pool halls, or in alleys. He is skilled enough to talk almost anyone out of almost anything. Even to list all the various con games would necessitate a separate volume. They require imagination, intelligence, and the intuitive ability to spot a sucker. One such con game is taking money with the promise of drugs or a prostitute but never returning. Were it not for the obvious enjoyment con men get from beating someone out of something for nothing, they would make excellent salesmen.

In the general description of their behavior patterns at least, such addicts most often fall under the psychopathic-personality category. Most of the basic functioning patterns are pretty much spread throughout all diagnostic categories, with more falling into the basic neurotic or basic psychotic than into the basic normal patterns. In other words, addicts may have a wide variety of psychiatric problems but do not fall neatly into one diagnostic category.

The Pimp and Prostitute Addicts

Very often several female addicts join one or more male addicts in an attempt to support their collective habits. The males may procure customers, or they may simply wait around to collect the money when the prostitute has finished. The function of the prostitute addicts, male or female, should be obvious. They rent their bodies for sexual use in return for money, sometimes to homosexuals, but more often to opposite-sex partners. Male procurers and male prostitutes (be they homosexual, heterosexual, or bisexual) more often are thought to have some kind of basic sexual deviancy than female prostitutes. The young female addicts may have very few alternatives if their habits are large, since they are usually unable to enter other kinds of criminal activities due to the lack of strength or nerve or both. With large habits they aren't able to work. To the non-drug world their functioning in the drug world would label them as amoral.

Procurement and prostitution come relatively easy to some addicts, but for those who come from comparatively straight (square or middle-class) backgrounds, such an existence can produce serious psychotic disturbances. The difficulty is that they are involved in two different kinds of illegal activity, sexual offenses and drug addiction. If an addict is arrested for a sexual offense, he may have to kick his habit "cold" (without medical assistance) in a jail cell. This is not an experience addicts look forward to, for kicking a heavy habit can produce cramps, runny nose, chills, vomiting, and diarrhea which can last from twenty-four to thirty-six hours.

The Thief Addict

Those who steal to support their habits tend to specialize. Some are shoplifters, others wander the streets at night and throw garbage cans through store windows (to steal merchandise), while those with means of transportation may go from the city to the richer suburbs, where they burglarize residences. Others specialize to the extent that they only hit all-night gas stations or liquor stores, or they stick to mugging individuals on the streets or in parks. The addict-thieves tend to be those less skilled in other ways of getting money, or those very "sick" (badly in need of a shot). The real effect of addiction on crime rates is not known with certainty. Not all addicts are habitual criminals, but it is difficult to find an addict who at one time or another hasn't resorted to crime to support his habit. It would seem safe to assume that drug addiction has been the largest single contributor to crime within the past twenty years. The numbers of addicts and crimes in major urban areas have increased at approximately the same rate.

All the activities of the addicts in the categories mentioned (the list is by no means exhaustive—pushers and dealers are very often users as well) have to do with behavior brought into play *after* the habit controls the person. My own experience with addicts is that very few are hard-core criminals. As a matter of fact, most are pitifully inept as criminals, and they tend to get caught sooner and more often than nonaddicted law violators. Professionals (other than pushers) in the various categories of criminal activity avoid addicts whenever possible, knowing them to be totally unreliable, and they very often heap scorn upon them, viewing their habit as a sign of weakness.

What does one describe as the dynamics of the addict? It will be helpful to look at the problem from a historical, individualized approach and to discuss predispositional factors, concomitant behaviors, and drug-free dynamics. Most of the predispositional factors have been discussed in some detail in the chapter on the addiction-prone person. They include a power imbalance in the family, or essentially a family background that tends to lead to schizophrenia in family members, and the other characteristics already described. The concomitant behavior described in this chapter represents illegal behavior other than drug addiction itself.

Drug-Free Basic Dynamics

It is possible to study the drug-free personality dynamics of an addict, but only in an institutional setting. The addict on the street is often inaccessible to the professional worker, and as a matter of habit he plays several different psychological games with anyone he comes into contact with. In an institution the former addict reverts to a level of functioning which combines his preaddiction personality with what remains of the way he lived as an addict. At times, but only under conditions of great trust, he will reveal some basic problems.

There are many times when the lowering of his defenses reveals a deeper level of sickness, such as a schizophrenic process. In such cases the visible problems are a thin veneer which disguises a basically schizophrenic condition that has never been allowed to express itself. At times it has been anesthetized by narcotics; the rest of the time it has been masked by the bravado of immature acting-out of anxiety. Most male addicts have the same ambivalent-dependency relationships with their mothers that is traditionally seen in male schizophrenics. The addict's confused state of psychosexual identity is also similar to the schizophrenic's state in many ways. Of course withdrawal by the addict under narcosis is more extreme than is that of the young schizophrenic alone in his room. Patterns of unusual psychological experiences, such as hallucinations, can be attributed to the effects of some drugs, both by the addict misusing these drugs and by the professional using them in an attempt to establish a firm diagnosis of the addict's mental and emotional condition. While the drug scene may at times be an escape from what might become severe mental illness, it must also be admitted that almost as frequently it can be an escape from what is an absurd, inconsistent, and often frightening reality for the individual who becomes an addict because he has no job, a miserable home, and only more poverty to look forward to. Whatever the addict is running from, whatever he thinks he is running toward, if he can ever become honest with himself (not an easy task for any of us), then he will have to admit that drugs are not an answer but a new set of questions.

The qualities most often uncovered are much more simple than one might expect. The addict who has opened up finally admits to being afraid—knowing that he is immature, but not knowing how to change that, feeling inadequate to holding up under pressures and requirements of job, family, and life in general. His most ironic and poignant desire is wanting so very much that "square" life addicts so often put down. And finally he admits to the awful feeling that once you are an addict, you can never really establish your place again in the larger society. Most addicts feel the road to addiction is a one-way street, for "nobody never really kicks for good until they're dead."

Love is the addict's greatest need and his greatest fear. To love requires trust, and people who have used others for their own ends and have never really given themselves to anyone find it nearly impossible to trust others enough to let themselves be loved. They continue, rather, to project their own lack of trust toward others and spend most of their time figuring out what the other person's "angle" is.

There are addicts who can turn around and leave drugs for good. But one very seldom sees them. They get jobs and move away, often as silently as possible. Their addicted friends no doubt think that they are in prison or that they finally died from an overdose. Exaddicts should make themselves more available and think about becoming counselors in the addictional programs being developed all over the country. The most impressive proof to an addict that he *can* kick his habit and make it in the straight world is to see an exaddict living a productive life.

5 : THE HARD-CORE ADDICT

Jim was born in a large northeastern city, one of five children, and grew up in a tenement section inhabited by first- and second-generation American families. It was never very easy for him at home or in the streets, but he showed no unusual behavior during his early years except a tendency to get into trouble at school a little more often than other kids. He had a basic sense of injustice, probably due to the way the family related to one another. His father was apparently the strong force in the family. He was a factory worker, very opinionated and not demonstrative in his affection for his wife and kids. Generally the mother tried to subvert his few attempts to reach his children, and she played the children against him. Jim always had a sense of dread, being unable to define what it was he sensed or what he feared with much accuracy. He only knew that the world seemed to be an unpredictable place in which the whims of others could change his life.

To escape the unpredictable atmosphere at home, Jim very early grew toward a street gang who made him feel that he belonged and was accepted. The group was a rather poorly defined one which changed from time to time to include as few as five or as many as twenty-five people. They were working into the "turf" that had for some time been the property of another gang. There were some fights, but mostly the gang existed to fill a void in the lives of its members. It was a family kind of feeling. Many of the original families were busy trying to make enough money to survive, or had broken up, or had simply failed to pay enough attention to their kids. There was some bravado about how many girls they had had and how tough they were, but Jim was never quite satisfied, even with all the fringe benefits of group membership.

One night after he had been introduced to wine and beer, an older group member sought out Jim and another boy and initiated them into the world of the junkie. ("Come on, man, you got to get with it. You got to be cool and try a real high for once!") They watched in wonder as the more experienced shooter emptied the contents of a small envelope into a bottle cap, cooked up with a match under the cap, drew it into a syringe, and tied up his arm with a belt. They watched with a mixture of fascination and fear while he probed to find a vein and, when some blood had backed up into the syringe, injected half the contents into his arm. He then turned both the younger kids on with a skin pop.

The feeling is difficult to describe, but it is one of almost total pleasure. All the bad feelings Jim had carried around seemed to melt away, and the result was a total kind of comfort he had never known before. He did not realize that he would shoot up a thousand times after that, looking for the same feeling. He didn't know you can't go home again, that you can never recapture that initial feeling. But he had just joined the international brotherhood of those who cannot feel, the artificial people with artificial feelings. It was too late to turn back now, because he had the feeling that he had finally found something he had been looking for, freedom from the constant gnawing fear and the conglomerate of other bad feelings.

He was introduced to petty thievery—purse-snatching and assorted con games. With the help of his friends he graduated to the streets and forgot about school, family, and most other human beings. At the age of fifteen Jim was arrested for breaking-and-entering and possession of narcotics. His stay of nine months in a juvenile detention home hardened his hatred of arbitrary authority figures, sharpened his hustling skills, and taught him new criminal activities to support his habit. He learned how to "jail" and all of the codes of behavior that went along with belonging to the wrong side of the law. He developed a fierce loyalty to other criminals and broke the last ties he had had with any straight people, including his family. In their indignation and shame they had disowned their son, and Jim seemed to be content without them. They had never really been there when he had needed them anyway.

His hardened exterior was all that he showed to the world. It is stupid to show your feelings to cops and foolish to tip your hand with other guys. The world became more and more dangerous, and he began to develop enough awareness about people to be able to smell out a sucker from a block away. It wasn't really very cool to get tied up with violence or in obvious criminal behavior like robberies. His taste developed more toward the subtle, like con games and running numbers. There was a long line of experiences that seemed to blend together with hustling, chasing the bag, and getting busted. A couple of times he checked into hospitals to kick the habit, because it was getting hot for him on the streets. He noticed that there seemed to be less and less pleasure from the drug, and by the age of twenty he was getting tired of the hassle. But he was still caught up in his own image. He couldn't break all the old habits that supported his addiction even if he could kick the drug physically. In effect they were the only trade he knew. But then he heard about a place like Synanon which helped junkies and was operated according to the concept of people banding together to help each other find another way of life, to search for meaning without the use of drugs.

At first Jim was cynical about his chances and about the possibility that anyone could really help him. His first trip to the house just about convinced him that he was right. They all ignored him. Even though he asked several times to see the man in charge, he was told to sit down and wait. When he was finally admitted, he was faced with four of the most hostile people he had ever seen. He couldn't con them or get by with anything. They loudly demanded total honesty and made it clear that they knew all the games from the streets better than he did. He left within minutes, but somehow he knew he would be back. He could not help trusting people who were so honest, and he very much wanted to trust somebody, for his life was cold and empty. He did come back, and this time he was determined that these people were not going to run him to the showers.

You couldn't really say that Jim actually bounced off the bottom of the barrel—and it was fortunate that he didn't. In the encounter sessions he was stripped of his old self-image and forced to rebuild a picture of himself that was realistic. The small amount of self-esteem he had salvaged provided some foundation. He was made to give up his street image, that of a tough, slick con artist. He was questioned by five former addicts, who fired questions at him like a machine gun. He felt his guts coming out. They told him to scream for help. They weren't convinced; he should shout louder. He did. Finally they were convinced, and then to his surprise they embraced him. He was in the door.

He polished the floors, scrubbed pots and pans, cleaned out the john, and toed the line for the first time in his life. He was beginning the long road to recovering many of the feelings and skills that he had lost, and it felt good. Nothing was being handed to him; he worked for what he got, and when he messed up, he heard about it. It took him about two years to go from the street to being a part of the management. He passed on what he had learned the hard way to the younger kids coming in off the streets, and he experienced the good feelings that come from knowing you have helped other people grow.

Finally he got a new set of feelings he had never known before: self-respect, a sense of accomplishment, and an awareness of the needs and rights of other people. He accepted speaking engagements in the community and stood up and recounted the story of his life. Not much of it was very pretty, except that the past two years had been good, very good. He was now well on his way to rejoining those people he had formerly called "square."

6 : THE COLLEGE "HEAD"

Ned was bright and precocious, and he had always been a little dreamy. He never achieved a tight family feeling with his parents. They were comfortable financially but never really at ease with each other. They were busy and were rather preoccupied with their separate lives, and they tried to give Ned all the better material things in life. They gave him toys and good food and shelter—and their attention when he did very well or very poorly in school. They wanted him to have the chance they had never had.

Ned progressed through the early grades, doing what was expected. He found it hard to concentrate, but he got good marks because the work was easy for him. He walked around his neighborhood a lot, and at night he would lie on the damp grass and look up at the stars. His mind wandered romantically—darting around harsh realities in search of something of beauty. He was considered a quiet, well-behaved kid. But then he did act a little strangely at times.

Ned always felt he had missed something somewhere from his parents. He had a feeling of being hungry for their touch and their attention. He wanted it more and more as time passed, because it was a need that was never met. When his father was at home, Ned reached out to him, but his father always seemed rather embarrassed. His mother was ashamed of her own need for physical contact and turned him away. They bought him things, but he never paid much attention to them. He dreamed of a world filled with warm and loving people. He was to look long and hard before he would find anyone who could understand, and in the meantime he came very near to not making it at all.

Ned's parents felt that a Catholic high school would prepare him best for college and also perhaps give him the self-discipline he seemed to lack. To a sensitive boy, it seemed a little harsh. The atmosphere was rigidly strict, and the boy still too compliant for any real compatibility, but finally he and the school accepted each other grudgingly.

His social life was slow at first. He played some basketball, but he was too short and not really quick or aggressive enough for the varsity team. However, there were a few kids who hung around together and who always felt a little bit on the edge of things . . . never really included, yet never really excluded. So he started hanging around with them. It seemed okay at first.

But every group finds some special thing that can be shared only by that group. One of the boys in high school had a connection, and he bought a couple of bags of pot. Ned sat in a circle one night and shared his high with a few other kids from the group. One girl got a little sick and lost her supper in the john. But most of the kids began to feel a little giddy and lightheaded. Marijuana was a groove they said.

Everyone began to giggle and talk fast and feel great —expansive and profound. For many people this is as close as they can come to really getting down to where it's at. For others it starts a long road, and they can't see what's ahead. It seems to depend on what else you have going for you. For Ned it was the beginning of a new chapter in his life. He liked pot. It cut him loose from his mind a little, which was fine with him. He wasn't too thrilled about living in his mind anyway.

Ned started on the path away from square people and toward drugs. Not everybody goes from pot to other drugs, but Ned did. He was already predisposed in that direction—a "head" doing his thing.

He met a girl while he was in college and his feeling of need came on more strongly. Both of them were really children, and it was easy to mistake need and contact and sexual arousal for love. They clung to each other against the stormy forces in their lives, but from the beginning they felt the hostility so common to people whose very life depends so strongly on another person.

He graduated from high school to college and from pot to acid. He dropped five hundred micrograms of LSD one night after his marriage, and it blew his mind. He had been in and out of college and couldn't really make his classes. Half the time when he did, he was high.

Then the babies started coming. His wife and later the kids provided the one constant in his chaotic life. He just wandered around a lot, and he finally ended up on New York's Lower East Side, where there was big drug traffic. Once his wife and kids left him, and he began to skin-pop heroin. He was a little beyond the head drugs, but this didn't seem to matter—the high was the thing. He got strung out, and he didn't like the junkie scene. It was tough, and he wasn't. He decided it was time to clean up and try to get his family back. It wasn't easy, but he did it, and they eventually moved to a smaller city. He was clean, so he took a couple of jobs. The jobs didn't seem to work out very well. He got bored very easily, and he was still discontented, even though his wife and kids were back with him. He knew he was egotistical, immature, and manipulative, but he also knew someone or something in him was struggling to come out.

He wandered around the city a little, looking for a different way to get involved. He found a place where people tried to help junkies, and he asked if he could help. He was able to get hooked up with several places, but the money wasn't much. He started drinking, and he got involved with junkies and tried to get some help for them.

But the frustration began to get to him. The state hospitals couldn't give him much help. He tried seeing a psychologist, but that didn't help either. He began to get invitations to speak with other exaddicts, but he was scared in front of large groups. He had to drink before the engagements, but he started getting deeper into drinking than he could handle.

Working as an exaddict with addicts still shooting stuff was hard for him. He felt *for* them, but he was pretty scared that he also still felt *like* them. He got in very tight with two other exjunkies who were slipping every now and then. It was too much for him, and by this time he was on the booze habit heavier than anything he had ever been on before.

His wife complained that he had no time for her and the kids. Since they had reconciled she had been trying hard to make it on the little bit of money he made. Even though he no longer shot drugs into his arm, the habit patterns of the junkie persisted. He felt he could not possibly attain anything through the normal pattern of work, achievement, and finally reward. Even when Ned intended to help others, his methods were such that everyone, including himself, ended up losing. It seemed that the drug habit itself was the easiest part to give up. His habits and language and style of life seemed even more deeply ingrained than his need for drugs.

Ned continued to work by the grace of his employer and the unwillingness of his co-workers, also exaddicts, to "rat" on him. Since drugs are illegal, drug-takers must mingle with the people on the street, so addicts take up the cops-and-robbers code.

Ned's relationship with his children was very important to him. He wanted them to know that they were loved (even though he seemed unable to show them), since he had never really felt loved by his own parents. He also wanted to be loved by them and would therefore never place limits on their behavior. But neither did he contribute any amount of time or work to taking care of them, and this made him feel guilty. He wanted his wife to love him and to accept his love, but he wanted nothing negative brought into the relationship. She also engendered guilt and for a time seemed to enjoy playing the martyr role and controlling her husband with his own guilt. He resented this control, but his need for her was so great that he wavered between seductive attention and hostile rejection. His wife found it hard to handle *any* kind of strong feelings.

Things went on like this until a relative sent plane tickets to her so that she and the children could leave him. This added a new dimension to the problem, for Ned and his wife were not good at making decisions. She had to attempt to give him some kind of an ultimatum, but her heart wasn't really in it. So she said, "I'd like to have you spend more time at home and not drink so much."

Ned didn't like being backed into a corner, and he had to respond without making any guarantees. He replied, "Look, I've been doing pretty good. I've only had six beers in three days, and no hard liquor at all. You've got to admit that's progress." It was progress, but his answer was a typical junkie curve ball. He had been asked to make some kind of statement about what he was going to do in the future. He switched this to a statement about the recent past, saying in effect, "See what a good boy I've been? Don't you feel you should reward me for what I've done?"

His wife's original statement had been given with little gusto, and she accepted the curve ball with apparent satisfaction. It got her out of the uncomfortable position of having to make the decision to leave, but by now the old behavior patterns they had developed had been reinforced.

Finally it became increasingly clear that Ned wanted his wife to go and take the children with her, but he was going to *force* her into making that decision. A coward right down to the wire. His drinking was sporadic, but he increased his promiscuous sexual behavior and passively let his wife find out about it. The cord was finally cut, and she took the children and left.

Ned still worked, and he continued to maintain the old habit patterns he had picked up while a "head" and during his short time as a junkie. Because his earlier self-preoccupation was rather intellectual, he had drifted toward the head drugs, pot and LSD. As he got in deeper, the junk helped him handle the visceral fear of finding himself unprepared in the streets. Finally he began to use alcohol so he could handle *all* kinds of feelings and still be able to function without getting arrested.

Ned was rather rare, in that most real "heads" stay away from both heroin and alcohol. But in changing his location from the campus to the street, he drifted with the tide of the external circumstances and took the easiest and safest form of escape.

At this point was Ned a "success" or a "failure" case? In many ways he was neither. It is impossible to categorize drug abusers so simply. Ned started abusing drugs in high school, and he continued to do so. He now abused a legal drug, alcohol, but his behavior patterns had changed very little since that first reefer. He had had so little experience with success that he tied his self-esteem very tightly to external events, and his actions were therefore determined by what he perceived from one minute to the next.

His capacities for intellectual achievement and interpersonal satisfaction lay dormant. He was stuck at one level of development, and unless he could perceive the need, he would never be able to face the desirability of changing that level. Having been down a number of roads, he could have been much more helpful in making this change. But as long as his manipulation of other people was periodically rewarded, it was not likely that he would see a reason to change. And there are always a significant number of people around who seem to enjoy being manipulated.

Ned reflects the current emphasis on "making it." His ethos was not remarkably different from that of many so-called "straight" people. Even his behavior was not a great deal different, in a society that rewards images instead of a deeper level of relating. He fit very nicely into the land of the disenchanted. He was at one with his world, but not with himself.

Ned had been backed into a corner by the circumstances of his life—the drugs had been bad enough, but his drinking got worse each day. His brief work experience with addicts fed his personal delusion that he knew "where it was at." A love affair with a half-desired woman provided an issue—he was at last forced to do something.

Ned made a trip to a self-help house. Although he was initially refused admission, he convinced the people there to let him in. The first months were very hard, but he stuck it out. He will probably make it now . . . but it has been harder for him than for most.

Now the question is not so much whether Ned will make it without resorting to drug abuse. It is more a matter of the larger question: can all of us strive for an atmosphere in which our human qualities and human dignity are prized above all else?

7: THE HIGH-SCHOOL EXPERIMENTER

Sue sat on the floor with her long straight hair drooping in front of her face. Behind the hair, tears were streaming down her face. It felt good to let go of the hurt and talk about how she had never really felt love until she started using drugs. She was talking about her early life.

"Our house was a place where a number of people lived, but not together. We were like zombies, passing in the hall like ships that pass in the night. I always saw the show we put on for ourselves and for other people. At parties there were smiles and words like dear and darling and sweetheart. But all I ever *felt* was hostility, resentment, and hatred. I think the fact that everyone thought I was pretty kept my mother satisfied for a while. But then when I was twelve or so, there were so many things I had to do which I didn't feel, and so many things I couldn't do which I felt were real, I began to feel unreal, like an object. I can remember seeing a strange smirk on people's faces when they talked that showed their words were a lie. I felt trapped and scared.

"When I was fourteen, I wanted to go to a party with a boy who had asked me. It set off a panic in the family. I didn't even know anything about sex, but they started to paint a picture of it for me. Mother screamed, 'Boys will say they love you and take advantage of you and leave you pregnant! All men are alike! They only want one thing!' It was all like a bad dream, because I didn't even know what she was talking about really. Oh, I knew about the birds-and-bees thing, but this picture of boys as monsters who were after my body was a little unreal. It just didn't fit this little kid that wanted to take me to the party. About that time I started to hate pretense and really went out to look for the love that I thought would save my life."

The group sat very still. They knew something about what she was saying because they had all experienced somewhat the same thing. It was a group for kids from a middle-class suburb who had gotten messed up with drugs and were trying to sort things out. It was being led by a psychologist who worked in the area and had volunteered two nights a week for the clinic set up by a local parents group. The kids sat on the floor in a circle. Sue was quiet now, and her face had a kind of calmness about it that came from trusting, from turning loose and allowing what you feel to flow toward other people.

"I think this needing to have someone hold me was almost constantly in my mind. I can remember going to the zoo and seeing two little monkeys clinging to each other. I can remember feeling envy for them, because I really wanted that myself."

A boy in the group spoke up. "It sounds like you were looking for someone to hold you like a baby. But that's not really love, is it? To me love means giving as well as getting."

The group first exploded at the boy for calling her a baby, and several of them said there was nothing wrong with wanting to be held. But Sue said, "You're right. I did want to be held and rocked like a baby, because I *felt* like a baby without any love. I still do in many ways. I think that is partly what smoking pot meant for me. I could feel things better, and the pain of loneliness was gone. And when someone held me, I didn't draw back like I did when I was straight. I can't really say that it was group pressure or a pusher or anything like that. I smoked pot at first because I was curious. I kept on smoking pot because it was the only way I could feel human. That was it."

Some group members smiled as they recognized that the word "baby" had hit a sensitive area for them. Then they related their own experiences, which were pretty much like those of Sue. It was something of a relief to be real, but it was also sad to realize that it took pot for them to feel human. Sue was given praise for being honest. She responded that she didn't really deserve the praise because she was just being real in order to hold herself together.

Sue had gotten to smoking pot heavily, and then she tried acid once. That was the turning point for her. She had a bad trip and panicked at her hallucinations. A girl who tripped with her appeared to have fangs and a green face. Sue saw a picture of a cat turn into a tiger. She was very frightened. She wanted that trip to be over more than anything in the world. She yelled and screamed for it to end. Her four-hour trip seemed to last four years.

After the trip Sue stayed away from drugs entirely for a couple of months. Then she tried pot again at a party one night, and she began to feel like she was on another trip. She started to feel the panic again. She didn't really know about "flashbacks" from acid, and she thought the pot was doing the same thing the acid had done. Flashbacks are spontaneous reoccurrences of the original trip that may happen up to a year later. Sue started to fear that she was losing her mind. It was about this time that she began to look for help.

Sue described to the group the kind of comfort she could experience when she was being real with people she trusted. When she or someone around her started to run some garbage, the feelings came back, like the fear that everything was an unreal dream. She said at this point she had no choice but to be real and that the praise she got was not truly deserved. The group seemed to understand. They usually seemed to understand, and that gave Sue a good feeling. She had begun to feel like a person again, and it felt good. She still felt anxiety, sometimes got depressed, and still had arguments with her parents and friends. She had not changed in many ways and still had much to work on, but for her, feeling real and human was a good place to start.

Sue is not very different from the black ghetto addict or the kid who ends up on barbiturates or speed or even alcohol. The way in which people talk about them may make their problems seem different, but basically we all seem to have the same kinds of problems. Sue and the members of her group had had problems before they got hooked on drugs. They will no doubt continue to have problems. But drugs become a problem in themselves, and one can work on his other problems much more effectively if he doesn't have to work on his drug problem at the same time. When you're stoned, you get the feeling that you are successful and brilliant and talented, but the feeling doesn't stay when the drug wears off.

Sue found a way to work on her drug problem. Now she is using the same method on her other problems. It seems to be working for her. Sue says the best part of the whole thing for her is that she enjoys the feeling of being able to help other people. That is a good feeling, which seems to stay around whenever you help people, and it doesn't take a drug to give you that feeling.

8 : FAMILY INFLUENCES

The family which gives birth to the drug addict is as deeply implicated in the problem of drug abuse as the society which houses that family. Since this is obviously *our* problem, we must all face it together. In the process perhaps we can admit to some of the very basic dilemmas which presently confront us. There are many historic roots of the problem, such as Victorian attitudes toward sexuality, the economic definition of man since the Industrial Revolution, and the failure of our society to absorb large minority groups. More than any other single force the double standard of morality is implicated. Presently we have one set of rules for adults and another for young people, and there is no clearly defined age at which one is no longer a child. From a historical point of view giving special status to children or adolescents or those of any other age is relatively new.

Since we have passed the pioneer survival stage as a nation, children have few functional roles. They no longer feel that they are useful as contributing members of a family unit. Middle-class children are often given money as a substitute for parental love or even for parental presence in the home. They have too much leisure time and very little sense of the relevancy of their own existence. Yet when their child begins to smoke pot, baffled parents ask what they did wrong. It is just that today parents seldom do anything younger people see as being right, such as loving them, spending time with them, teaching them, working and playing with them, and telling them what it means to be human and to create order out of chaos and how to create meaning in the face of absurdity.

The areas of similarity in the family of the addict should be established, for the family which may have created an addict has much in common with many other families in the social, cultural, and geographic context of their own world. One family may contain an addict, another an alcoholic, another an individual with chronic anxiety or depression. Assigning the guilt is not important to the problem as a whole. What is relevant is, who contributes what to the problem of drug abuse?

Measuring a man by economic standards is clearly a part of our current American ethos. If a person makes little or no money, he is seen as being less successful, or weaker, or lazier than others, or as all of these. If he makes more money, he is seen as being bigger, stronger, or more successful than others, regardless of his methods or his morals. This obviously puts those who are behind in the economic race still further behind in the eyes of their families. Some minority-group men who may be passive or unable to compete successfully for any reason are seen as less than they "ought" to be (see Chapter 10, "Cultural Influences"). And since money, or the lack of it, is the most popular subject for family arguments, the husband, defined economically, is made impotent if he cannot earn money.

This leads to a power imbalance in the family if the wife gains ascendancy at the expense of her husband. Both the arguments and the imbalance are usually sensed as being subversive by the children in such a family. If the mother adds manipulation of the children as a tool to defeat further her staggering husband, the children may feel more and more like *objects*, being bounced back and forth between the two for reasons they don't understand, and less and less like *people*. It should be emphasized that the power imbalance, the inconsistency, and the manipulation may be present without the economic defeat, so any income level can show this kind of family process. When the children approach adolescence, a family in such disorder faces more dilemmas. Sexual maturity generally predates sexual experience in our culture, so many types of sexual aberrations can result from this type of conflict.

A family so directed by outside mores as to accept the absurdities and inconsistencies of a status system based upon income is also very likely to accept sexual prohibitions as well—and for children who have been depersonalized, sexual gratification may be their last best hope. The predictable "damned if you do and damned if you don't" double-bind result is to place young people in a trap they do not comprehend—and in a search for anything that will allow them to escape.

So the family of the addict is the end result of the many complex forces deeply imbedded in our culture, and they are also deeply imbedded in the addict, to the point of being virtually invisible to us. In the process of group or individual psychotherapy, these recurring themes have been repeated again and again, with the variations on these themes being unusual. The consistency of their pattern is rather startling in contrast to the many ways people get labeled as "sick" in other psychiatric categories, but the overlap of the pattern of interaction of the addict's family with the family of the schizophrenic is also quite clear. Research on the pattern of interaction among families of schizophrenics has turned up similar results.

The difference between the various patterns of symptomatology (addict, alcoholic, or schizophrenic) and the original family dynamics seems to have been left to more or less accidental intervening influences that are separate from the family and have to do with the life experience of the individual involved. The description of the addiction-prone person in Chapter 1 is clearly related directly to this pattern of family interaction, but as it was indicated there, the addiction-prone individual may or may not become addicted.

What should be done when one family member discovers that another family member is playing with drugs? When this happens, one should find out all he can about what need is being filled by the drugs and see if that need can be filled in other ways. He should seek professional advice, and most important, he should discuss everything that is relevant with the individual involved. Evasion and moralism will not make it—he must examine everything and everyone involved as honestly and openly as he can; otherwise, he will simply be adding to the problem.

9 : PEER GROUPS

Each of us makes a few tentative explorations out of his family circle very early in life. There are some rather well-defined first steps, such as the first day at school, the first time away from the family overnight, the first trip with other than family members, and finally the first full breakaway to school, the service, or one's own apartment.

In between there are groups which are more or less formal that influence the life of the individual. Any group from nursery school to the local Lions Club could be considered a peer group, but those most relevant to drug abuse are street gangs and informal school groups that eventually lead to the drug subculture itself.

There are those who never quite make it into the gang, and there are those who don't need it. But the addiction-prone person needs the gang. He has been depersonalized and has bounced around, and he seeks a substitute family that will accept him as he is. That person needs *any* group of more than three who will admit him, praise him, allow for his growth, and guarantee his protection, in whatever form it comes. If a person has nothing to belong to, any group will be better than none.

The names these gangs choose are irrelevant. And the form, purpose, and degree of their acceptability or inclusiveness or exclusiveness with regard to the larger society may be accidental. The degree to which they choose drugs as an expression of their needs may also be accidental.

There are two conditions which must exist before groups can lead individuals to drug use. First of all the group must serve the addiction-prone individual as a substitute family. Second, drugs must be both available to and approved by the group. Both of these conditions are very often being met by peer groups. The very fact of their existence is usually a testament to their need as a substitute for needs formerly filled by the family. In the attempt to compensate for a lack of solidarity and discipline within the family, peer groups characteristically overstructure their relationships and overdiscipline their members.

Indeed substitute family organizations, such as Synanon, which are devoted to the rehabilitation of the exaddict, seem to overstructure status relationships and to undervalue people even more flagrantly than their families or their former peer groups, in many cases.

The more deficient the family, the more compensatory is the peer group. The more deficient the peer group (including the drug subculture), the more structured and primitive is the substitute for the drug "family." The original deficiency in good family feeling requires that the members of a substitute family overstructure their own lives in an effort to rebuild the family function later in life.

Very often rehabilitation professionals are also overstructuring their programs, perhaps as a compensatory mechanism for the deficiencies in their families, peer groups, or supporting relationships. There seems to be a spiral effect involved; that is, the initial difficulty is made worse by subsequent efforts toward a "cure."

A street gang is a pale imitation of a strong family. The drug subculture is a pathological substitute for the gang, and too often the "curative" institutions or agencies are in more chaos than *any* of the preceding groups. One would assume that a substitute group might be better able to satisfy the needs of members than the original dysfunctional group. But the opposite seems to be true; that is, the Mafia, the school gang, or the Elks seem to fill fewer and fewer of the needs of their members as compared with the original family unit. This is seldom expressed directly by any group member—verbally that is, but their behavior would indicate otherwise.

When one invests any group, or a number of them,

with the primary influence in one's life, then the groups preceding the present one in time must have failed to one degree or another to retain primacy. The primary needs for safety, affection, and nurture were either being underfilled or overfilled, so the next group gained more primacy at the expense of the family or other previous groups.

These groups may gain, and subsequently lose, primacy in their determination of behavior over a period of time. Furthermore, whether or not a family or some later group is able to meet the primary needs may depend on a combination of the particular group's ability to meet such needs and the individual member's level of such needs, along with his perception of how his needs are being filled. That is, the family may meet the needs of every family member except one.

Several things are involved in regard to which addiction-prone person picks which group, but most of them are related to ethnic and socioeconomic status. The kids who grow up on the streets and are black or of Spanish extraction usually break away and pick street gangs sooner than middle-class whites. Their chances of staying in school and maintaining some measure of acceptability in the school setting have been reduced by the economic, cultural, and social values generated in the society at large. With those who choose school or campus groups to fill their needs, the fact that they have delayed their escape enhances the extent of their break with the mores of the original family. It may become necessary for one's long-delayed personal revolution to go to extremes to make up for the feeling of having been used for so long. It may take the form of drinking bottles of codeine cough syrup in junior high school, or smoking pot in high school, or drinking wine or beer, or wearing long hair and hippie clothes. The particular form it takes is almost irrelevant. Those who feel the greatest amount of discomfort will likely choose drugs that serve two purposes—comfort and rejection of the authority of others. Those who experience less anxiety or depression will likely choose the more visible evidence of their alienation—dress and hair length.

At times addicts admit that after their first run with a drug, it began to lose effect as their body built in some tolerance to the drug, but by that time they were caught up in the game and had met several friends who were also users. They valued the friends more than the drug, and even when they were tired of the drug, they continued to use it to keep these friends. It is tragic when a person has to resort to drugs, or to a lonely hearts club, just to meet some friends. One addict reported that he began to do dumb things, like buying heroin during the day on the street, rather than at night out of sight in an alley, just to get arrested. He said that he didn't know anybody in the streets, but that when he got to prison, he was greeted by name:

"Hey, John, they caught you again, huh?"
"Yeah, that's the way it goes, right?"
"I know what you mean!" He laughs.

Now he was back with the "family" again, even though he was behind bars and in uniform and had no freedom. At least there they knew his name. Sometimes *any* group can fill an individual's needs, as long as he can eat and have a place to sleep and people don't yell at him too much. This is difficult to understand for those who have had the comfort of family solidarity and have never felt constant emotional pain in their guts, but it happens—and more often than one might expect.

Such simple needs—affection, safety, nurture, stability—and yet if they are not filled within the first fourteen or fifteen years, the scars will always remain and the needs will never fully be met. One can perhaps arrange for some partially suitable substitutes, but they will still only be substitutes.

10 : CULTURAL INFLUENCES

Public agencies which serve drug addicts should have persons from several kinds of disciplines on their research staffs, but the one which is always missing is the cultural anthropologist. This is a serious omission, for what a person becomes is very often a function of his cultural milieu compounded by later family and social conditions.

The notion implicit in such a statement concerns behavior being determined by the situation as opposed to self-determined behavior. This must be made clear in order to provide a framework for the observations which follow. People seem to have a great need to proclaim personal control over their behavior as a function of their need for individuality, the *bête noire* of Western man, but the intensity of their proclamations often seems to be inversely proportional to their actual ability to retain this control. The more a person insists that he make all his own decisions and determine his own behavior, the more he seems to be controlled by external circumstances.

Black Americans

The black American has been accurately depicted by Thomas F. Pettigrew in his book *A Profile of the Negro American.*

The culture of the African was to a large extent supplanted by the practices of slave traders and slave owners during the two hundred and forty-four years after 1619, when the first Negro slaves had been forcibly brought to the English colony at Jamestown, Virginia. Families and tribal groups were split up, and little continuity of culture could be expected under such conditions. This was the case until recently, when black Americans began to take a renewed interest in their African heritage. Currently there is also a great interest in the *American* heritage of blacks, although this interest has met great resistance from many educators.

The culture of the black American was built largely in the South, where they existed in the largest numbers. For most of them, it includes, among other things, soul food, music, religion, dance forms, and fairly well-defined mores. For smaller groups it has included intellectual, financial, and political achievements. The situation is much more fluid today, and it has been historically changing rapidly since the inception of the civil-rights movement.

Most blacks born in the South who took the chance of getting something better in the larger cities of the North and the Midwest and on the West Coast didn't always find that something on their arrival. Many of them have still not found it.

The family structure of the slave family was an enforced matriarchy (or was at least matrifocal). The mother tried to keep her children as best she could. The father could be sold or traded particularly easily and often was. After emancipation the economic definition of the black man began to do as much psychic damage to him as it eventually did to white men and to those of all ethnic groups.

Since the turn of the century in America, the larger white society has considered the black man less employable than the black woman, who could if all else failed at least depend upon domestic service. Although the situation is now beginning to improve, the inequities have been burned into the consciousness of black people, particularly those under thirty or thirty-five.

Many black families in America try very hard to keep the father in ascendancy. But neither wife nor children are able to produce the job that isn't there or turn a father's acceptance of things "as they are" into aggressive action to change them, although there is now far less of this passive acceptance than previously, particularly among young people.

Puerto Ricans

This group is being considered separately from other Spanish-speaking groups because of their recent large emigration to the United States and their current status as a group that is still not accepted by the larger community. Oscar Lewis, in *La Vida,* outlines well the culture of poverty in San Juan and New York and the difficulties faced in each setting, as well as those attributable to the change of location.

The historic family structure in Puerto Rico was strictly patriarchal until recent times. The economic rebirth of the country since the 1950's has affected family structure and function. The poor farmer in the remote provinces could maintain his ascendancy with subsistence farming and a strict hand. But transplanted to San Juan or Spanish Harlem the family fared less well. The mother and the sisters could do needlework, for example, but the males, unprepared for urban life, often became family liabilities. In the past if the father could find another place to live, the family was able to get some welfare assistance, at least in many metropolitan areas.

Other Ethnic Minorities

The Mexican-American in the Southwest and West of the United States has many of the characteristic Latin qualities of the people from the Caribbean. They differ by having a slightly stronger tie to religion, a little richer cultural tradition, and admixtures with indigenous Indian peoples (rather than the Negroid admixtures found among Puerto Rican Americans). Their lack of vocational skills and English is often just as serious a handicap as it is for Puerto Ricans.

The American Indian has also been a chronic loser in the economic race and has had the additional liability of being, in effect, a ward of the federal government on what remains of his own land tracts. Other minority groups have been to a greater or lesser extent included or excluded from the economic race for a wide variety of reasons.

The cultural heritage of each minority group may be the solid substratum of family functioning and therefore a strengthening influence, or it may be the basis for isolation and possible disintegration. The key factor seems to be how well the family is able to function within its own home, separate from the extraneous intervening influences outside its front door. Two strong parents who function well within the family circle can offset the many negatives encountered by the children during the course of a day.

It is a little more devastating on the negative side. Regardless of other influences, the family that does not pass on to its children a strong cultural heritage, in whatever form it may take, runs the high risk of producing persons with no sense of their own past. Whatever the religion, the occupation, or national origin involved, it is vital for people to feel that they are an extension of some kind of tradition. Otherwise they are forced to relate themselves to a historical void.

Very often people with emotional problems can't even recall their own pasts, let alone what their grandparents did. A sense of time requires an awareness that the present is the extension of the past and the prelude to the future. This is quite important, since addiction-prone people want everything *now* and without effort. With a tradition to follow, one can afford to make investments today that will not pay dividends until some future date.

Since man is the only animal who can know his collective past and attempt to anticipate his future, he can assume that the moment presently available to his conscious awareness has a quality that is the result of man's continuity. But this assumption does not hold up for the addict. Lack of ego development does not allow the addict to sense continuity. If one's superego, or awareness of the rules of society, is soluble in alcohol, then one's ego can be retarded by drugs.

If you began to shoot heroin at the age of twelve and continued until you were thirty, which would not be unusual, you would not only have failed to learn about your own cultural heritage, you would also have bypassed all the other problems that nonaddicts had already worked out. In effect you would be a twelve-year-old living in the body of an adult.

It should be emphasized that minority-group status in America tends to make an individual more profoundly affected by economic and social inequities. The families of minorities do not function poorly because they belong to a minority, but because they are subjected to more of the damaging pressures that affect all poor families, which are added to the general problems bearing on all families in our society. Minority-group status does not in and of itself predispose family members to drug addiction. It can be said that all forms of disabilities, physical and psychological, occur in low-income housing areas and ghettoes. This is an indictment of our society's unequal treatment of low-income people in social, economic, and health aspects, rather than of the families and individuals who find themselves victims of this system.

Heroin addiction is also rising rapidly in middle- and upper-income families which are not continually subjected to the additional pressures experienced by low-income families. In the middle-class addict, it is usually much easier to find contributing factors in the individual and the family rather than in the societal pressures mentioned earlier in this chapter. The first group of negative influences on addiction-prone persons has its causation on a social level. This level is the most obvious, for it is applicable to large numbers of people who belong to a group that is subject to the same societal pressures, such as minority group members living in a ghetto. The second level of causation of negative influences is the dysfunctional pattern of family interaction, which was discussed previously. The third level of causation of negative influences, like the social level, also has its causes primarily outside the home. This final level is the life experiences of a person that are separate from those of his family.

In attempting to isolate the cause of drug behavior, one must remember that any behavior has many contributing causes.

11 : MEDICAL ASPECTS

One of the most ironic aspects of drug addiction is that the disease is sometimes caused by too much of the cure. As was pointed out earlier, until recently there have been some appropriate medical uses for morphine. Heroin was in earlier times hailed as the "cure" for addiction to other opiates. Currently, methadone, a synthetic narcotic, is being used both for withdrawal from heroin by gradually reduced dosage and for continued maintenance until other methods of treatment such as psychotherapy, education, or vocational training can effect a significant change in the addict's personality.

Very often people become medically addicted to drugs, and sometimes addicts use heroin as a self-administered psychiatric medication. The tragedy in these cases is that they could get better treatment and be able to control their feelings more effectively and legally if they got the help of a competent psychiatrist or psychotherapist. Psychiatric medication should not be self-administered or self-regulated. But there are several difficulties in this rather straightforward statement.

Few people fill the cavities in their own teeth, and fewer still, if any, take out their own appendixes. However, at present, many people seem to be their own psychiatrists or psychologists. The how-to-do-it self-analysis books, the availability of the works of Freud, and several other varieties of the "instant cure" have helped many people to avoid treatment. The stigma associated with psychiatric care has not disappeared, and thus addicts would rather face prison than admit they need professional help in understanding their feelings. This seems extremely stupid, but in many cases it is true. In addition the manipulative aspects of being caught up in a subset of the cops-and-robbers game are involved, and the drug subculture acts as a substitute family for the addict.

Heroin, like alcohol, is a depressant to the central nervous system. It is a mild anesthesia and, depending upon the dosage and the predisposition of the individual when he takes it, may simply relieve felt anxiety or depression or produce a moderate euphoria. Being high is in many ways a misleading term in that with stronger doses the addict nods or nearly goes to sleep.

In small doses the drug masks fatigue, and it may therefore produce a temporary lift in spirits, but again like alcohol in large doses it eventually produces a depressing effect and eventually sleep, in some cases of overdose, or "O.D.," permanent sleep.

A wide variety of drugs is used for the detoxification of addicts. The choice of drug is based upon the general state of health, the size of the habit, and the kind of drug the addict was using. The addict doesn't eat when he can use that money for junk, so a high-calorie, high-protein diet is sometimes prescribed (under the best treatment conditions), along with vitamin supplements in some cases.

The difficulty is that most often the best treatment conditions are not available to the addict. General hospitals don't want the addict, because they fear he will break into the narcotics cabinet and then escape. State mental hospitals generally don't want him either, because so many come into the hospital only to reduce the size of their habits and usually leave too early, before any other meaningful treatment has begun. If addicts are involved in group or individual psychotherapy, they often know the game so well that they say what they think the therapist wants to hear. Convinced that these addicts are cured, the staff discharges them, only to get them back in a month or two. The feeling of having been had, or conned, is not a comforting one for professionals who are supposed to be the experts. The predictable result is that they reduce the number of addicts admitted and screen them carefully. To give a balanced picture, it should be said of the professional therapists involved that they are often extremely manipulative individuals themselves, and they don't like the competition which the addict gives them, most especially when the addict wins the verbal con game more often than they do. Our Puritan heritage also comes to the surface, with both addicts and alcoholics, when the professional staff feels that since the drug addict or alcoholic experienced some kind of pleasure in what he did, he *deserves* the pain he experiences during withdrawal. This is akin to the case of the unwed mother who is given nothing for pain during childbirth to "teach her a lesson." Those who don't follow the rules in our society very soon experience the implicit reward-and-punishment system that operates in addition to our actual laws and professional ethics.

Many addicts, since they are usually medically indigent, have little choice but to submit to whatever treatment they are given, since it often takes place together with some form of incarceration. Physicians and psychiatrists do have a choice, but they seldom seem willing or able to provide adequate care, for the reasons previously stated. Some of the reasons are easy to understand, but in no case are they ethical.

Pain is pain, whether it comes from a tumor, an infected wound, or a drug habit. Physicians are ethically bound to relieve pain. They sometimes do not do so when drugs or alcohol are involved, and in such cases, they are reacting in an unethical, judgmental, and punitive manner and are not then deserving of the respect society generally affords them.

Drugs are meant to treat pain and should be used in

most cases of addiction and without the "as indicated" escape clause. A heroin addict who is being maintained on Dolophine or methadone for pennies a day does not have to steal up to one hundred and fifty dollars a day to support his habit. In addition the person who is maintained in such a fashion is under medical control and surveillance, is able to control feelings well enough to participate in other treatment, rehabilitation, and educational activities, and is gaining enough self-esteem to be able to function as a member of society.

Dolophine may not always be the drug of choice, true, but *some* drug to offset the pain of withdrawal, and perhaps a different drug for the continuing control of feelings, is most often indicated. Addicts need the best medical care, but like the poor most often get the worst.

American physicians may defend their behavior in not treating addicts appropriately by pointing to the "failure" of the British system, where individual physicians may prescribe narcotics or substitute narcotics legally. They point with alarm to the rising number of addicts in Britain, from two or three hundred to slightly more than eight hundred, a statistic largely limited to one section of London. There are as many as eight hundred addicts in one square block in some sections of New York City.

These physicians seem to forget what happened during Prohibition, when we made alcohol illegal and thereby created a black market in alcohol traffic and consumption. It is clear that as a nation we learned nothing from Prohibition. It is not possible to legislate morality, whether it concerns drugs, alcohol, or sexuality. Yet we continue to try to do so and to witness the devastating effects of "crime in the streets." We helped put it there by trying to enforce a normative middle-class set of values through laws which are virtually unenforceable.

12 : LEGAL ASPECTS

There aren't any easy answers in regard to drug addiction. There aren't even any easy questions, but it is usually clear that when existing laws and approaches to treatment are not working, we should try to restructure them. In my opinion present laws and treatment programs very often make the problem worse.

If an addict leaves prison, a state mental hospital, or another institution where treatment is poorly conceived and administered, he feels justified in returning to his habit. The institution justifies his feeling that authorities are uninformed and inconsistent. He also feels justified in convincing other active addicts to keep their habits. As bad as the habit might be, he says, it is to be preferred to the treatments he has received.

The average legislator knows little about drug addiction, but he does have a well-established habit pattern. This is a problem that local communities cannot handle, whether it affects those suffering from mental retardation, mental illness, alcoholism, or drug addiction. Sixty years ago nearly every small town had its village idiots, its "peculiar" citizens, its town drunks, and those people who needed more drugs than others. Somehow we were able to exist during those years, and people made allowances for such citizens. But with our progress and sophistication about such matters (advances in science, technology, etc.), we now pass laws against these people, place them in institutions, and feel that we have done them a beneficial service.

Again, to balance the picture, in some cases we do provide real and valuable services. The acutely psychotic housewife may have to stay in a modern community mental-health center only overnight and will then be maintained as an outpatient for several months, with good care. The retarded child may receive day services and education with his peers to prevent his having to leave home. And the elderly senile man receives much better care in a modern state hospital than he could get in most other settings.

But drugs constitute the first epidemic in history which has been ignored for so long. In addition, drugs have compounded the usual generation gap into a Grand Canyon, and when superimposed upon the general revolution in social and moral values currently in progress, drugs constitute a clear and present danger to social progress.

The laws themselves are currently still oriented to some combination of punishment (prison) and a treatment program which is usually added as an option of the judge. If you have to incarcerate someone in order to treat him, you are building a large negative factor into your program before beginning. It is the popular opinion that *no* addict will voluntarily seek help unless he has a charge pending against him or is threatened by his family. It is true to this extent: Most addicts won't volunteer (unless they just want to reduce their habit) for programs where there is little chance of being helped to any significant degree to stay off drugs. Because most current programs do not help them stay off drugs, they don't volunteer. They may be addicted, but they are not stupid.

The underground grapevine among addicts is more efficient in transmitting news than a radio station. If we passed an effective law which did not involve incarceration, set up an effective treatment program, and helped most people stay off drugs entirely (and maintained the remainder on synthetic narcotics until they *could* stay off), people would line up for treatment every day.

It should be understood by legislators, lawyers, and policemen that drugs in themselves are not either good or bad, just as the people who use or misuse them are neither good or bad by virtue of their using or misusing drugs. The poppy and the *cannabis sativa* plant (marijuana) are called "illegal." But a plant cannot be either legal or illegal; it merely exists. This is analogous to calling an elm tree illegal because some person might cut it down, make part of it into a baseball bat, and beat somebody's brains out with it. And would it still be illegal if a baseball player were hitting home runs with it?

Legislators are charged with making laws that will promote our safety and interests and our common welfare. If this tradition is to be uniform, it must truly include all people, not just those in vested-interest groups. Addicts and alcoholics must first be considered a part of us all. Then we may be in a position to help them and indirectly the rest of society.

I am not of the opinion that laws will help, other than those which provide a great deal of money for good treatment programs. I think the current arguments about legalizing marijuana or LSD, or whatever, are largely specious in terms of having a direct effect on the pattern of drug usage. These drugs are being used now —legal or illegal. Therefore the *direct* effect of laws on drug use would seem to be tenuous at best.

The more relevant question might be why we need to use (or rather misuse) such substances? When did we lose track of those qualities which helped us to get our kicks from the struggle of working, loving, and living? Why is satisfaction from doing a job well becoming obsolete? Why are good craftsmen, good artists, and good artisans becoming a vanishing breed? If you are asking what connection there is between the preceding questions, you not only don't know the answers, you are a part of the problem.

We seem to be a nation of hustlers. Drug addicts

simply reflect this national tendency like a mirror, and we reject them because we reject our own image.

What makes a solid citizen out of a hustler? Caring . . . about himself and others . . . makes the difference. You cannot legislate morality, nor can you legislate caring.

The next generation of laws about drugs, alcohol, and sexuality between consenting adults will largely consist of passing nonpunitive legislation along with providing money to help people who have problems, regardless of the nature of their problems. At least this is what will happen if we care enough about ourselves and others on a basic human level to want to *help* instead of punish.

13 : REHABILITATION PROGRAMS

Rehabilitation programs designed exclusively for heroin addicts have been developed largely during the past decade. The federal government established one of the first hospitals in Lexington, Kentucky, in 1935. At present only two states, California and New York, have statewide programs with a full range of services coordinated through a separate state agency.

The other states establish their own drug laws and therefore their own programs, most of which are administered by a department of health. Usually some combination of incarceration and treatment is provided for in these program. If treatment exists, it may often take place within a penal institution. Some laws leave the judge the option to remand the addict to the commissioner of mental health (or equivalent title within the state) for care, usually for a treatment period of a specified length. If charges other than drug use are involved, they may be held up pending the treatment outcome or dropped.

The Narcotics Addiction Rehabilitation Act passed by Congress in 1966 provides for a thirty-day diagnostic period in a federal institution, after which a report is sent back to the federal judge at the local level. The United States attorney at the state level gets both the voluntary applications and the cases of people which involve drug-related charges. The strong point of this program is that the addict who comes back into his local community is automatically a client of the state–federal vocational rehabilitation program. This program is able to purchase many kinds of services that can help the exaddict achieve maximal vocational adjustment. This could be anything from an eight-week training program to a college education.

Other programs throughout the country take several forms, with either a medical, mental-health, vocational, or educational emphasis. The difficulty is in finding a program which contains *all* of these components and which uses former addicts as counselors. A truly comprehensive program must contain all of these components, but the state program must be placed somewhere within the structure of the state government. Where it is placed to a large extent determines what the emphasis of the program will be. The politics of bureaucracy is such that when a commissioner brings in different kinds of components, it will usually be by way of hiring professionals from the category under *his* direct control, rather than using professionals from other agencies or institutions on a sharing basis. The difficulty in this arrangement is that the general direction of the program at the policy-making level seldom gets new kinds of perspectives on adapting the program to a constantly changing set of needs. A psychiatrist working at a college will work differently than when working for a prison. The habit patterns (and indeed thought patterns) of individuals working inside any agency for more than five years generally become homogenized. Tradition and policy restrict the use of new ideas. There may be a certain amount of new blood coming into the agency periodically, but unless it is at a level high enough to affect policy, the agency program remains intact, and the inbreeding caused by promoting strictly from within results in a sterile program.

Since drug addiction programs are most often placed within a bureaucratic structure, the dynamics of bureaucracy are very relevant to the design of these programs. A carefully designed plan to combat drug abuse inevitably depends upon the competence of the people chosen to run it, and choosing people who are flexible helps. It will also help to pick people who are comfortable enough in their own professions to see the value in other professions.

A number of new approaches have been tried in rehabilitating drug addicts. One good review of such programs was published in 1967 by the United States Government Printing Office, under the auspices of the Vocational Rehabilitation Administration (*Rehabilitating the Narcotics Addict*). This volume contains reports from federal and state programs and from several research and demonstration projects funded by the Vocational Rehabilitation Administration (which, under the Social and Rehabilitation Service Administration Department of the Department of Health, Education and Welfare in Washington, D.C., has been renamed the Rehabilitation Services Administration) and other federal agencies. (See list, page 149.) The programs may include several services, and each program may cover all or only a few of these services.

Intake : Whatever the source of referral or motivation, verification that the individual is addicted to heroin or a related drug is usually required. Most programs for addicts are not currently set up to handle the drug-dependent person on non-narcotic drugs, since so many active addicts are in need of their services. In addition some testing and evaluation is done to establish what kinds of services seem to be indicated, beyond medical detoxification, to assist the addict in his efforts to be self-sustaining following rehabilitation.

Detoxification : In chronological order detoxification is actually concurrent with intake or precedes it, since the addict must be relieved of the pain of withdrawal symptoms before any other step can take place. The drugs used for detoxification depend not only on the height and weight of the addict and the length and dosage size of his last "run," or habit since the last time without drugs, but also on the individual physician who supervises his detoxification and the policies of the treatment facility. Most current programs seem to vary, from using no drugs ("cold turkey") to giving inappropriately high dosages.

Treatment : This may include any or all of the therapeutic forms used with patients in other psychiatric categories, including group and individual psychotherapy; counseling; milieu therapy (or therapeutic community); recreational, educational, and occupational therapy; and, at times, vocational training. All of the therapeutic forms mentioned (or any combination) may be considered treatment. The treatment, however, is usually designed, implemented, and supervised from the viewpoint of the professional. The particular program carried out will depend upon the experience and training bias of the director. It is rare when a program includes a recipient of the services as part of the policy-making machinery. Drug addicts who are drug-free are at least capable of telling professionals which program components are *not* working. But professionals in human-services areas seldom even listen to professionals working in areas near their own, let alone to the recipients of their services.

Placement : For the addict who has undergone treatment, either a job or a particular kind of follow-up setting (such as a halfway house) is very important. An addict who must return to the same setting and who has no real friends aside from other addicts and pushers needs a great deal of strength to avoid old habit patterns. The strength or weakness of any program therefore rests upon the effectiveness of the follow-up stage.

Follow-Up : During this stage of rehabilitation, well-trained counselors coordinate other services in the community and support the exaddict in his efforts to readjust his habit patterns to a new setting. The knowledge that a particular person is available as needed or on a regular basis can be very helpful to the exaddict, assuming that the exaddict feels this person wants to help. Suspicions and doubts transmitted by such a counselor can be as harmful as the doubts of the exaddict in himself. The official title or professional status of the counselor matters less than his intent; that is, whether he is trying to help or is looking for the exaddict's weaknesses. My experience indicates that people usually find what they look for in others, whether it is weakness or hidden potentials for growth.

Rehabilitation programs for exaddicts have evolved only in recent years. Before that these people were considered hopeless. In an article entitled "New Horizons in the Treatment of Narcotic Addiction" by M. H. Diskind, which appeared in the December 1960 issue of *Federal Probation,* several studies with success rates of over forty percent were reported. And an article in the April 1958 issue of the *Bulletin of the Los Angeles County Medical Association* ("How 92% Beat the Dope Habit" by L. E. Jones) reported a study with a ninety-two percent success rate. In these studies "success" was defined as being drug-free for a given follow-up period.

The most viable theory concerning former addicts giving up all drugs is based on the accumulation of small rehabilitating experiences over a period of time that will serve to keep the individual drug-free. By age thirty-five or forty the addict who has not yet died of an overdose has bounced in and out of correctional or mental-health institutions and other programs, and he either has been able to accumulate enough ego strength or has simply gotten tired and given up the struggle.

Some combinations of the program components mentioned, if taken together, would constitute a good program. But this would take a great deal of money and understanding support from public agencies and from the public at large.

14 : SYNANON

Synanon was founded in California in the 1950's by Charles Deiderich, a former alcoholic. It has grown and evolved into a social movement in which each "house" is a self-contained unit which supports itself within the larger community. Extreme community pressure to move out has been exerted on many houses, but in spite of such pressure (or perhaps because of it in some cases), the idea has spread in scope.

The basic idea involves a community of individuals who band together and confront each other daily with stupidity (Mr. Deiderich's word) that allows them to continue their maladaptive and self-destructive habits. This is done through regular encounter–confrontation group sessions. In addition a meeting may be called at any time by any resident of a Synanon house for the purpose of straightening out problems that arise between regular meetings.

The original Synanon houses were partially supported by private donations but largely through the outside work of their individual members during the day. In its original form such a living arrangement used to be called "apartment-house socialism," because each member contributed to the common welfare of all.

An addict who entered a Synanon house was allotted a short time to kick his habit without assistance. Since all the house members had been through the same experience, very little sympathy was available from them. As a general rule they tended to let the addict know that acting like he was going through the tortures of hell was just so much garbage to them. This general atmosphere prevailed. ("Don't give us this crap, because we invented the game you're playing!") This brutal honesty prevailed later as well, when neophytes were assigned to menial jobs—cleaning out the bathrooms, sweeping and mopping the floors. A very rigid status system was maintained, with titles like Chief Expediter and Assistant Chief Expediter. Those who were senior in job title or seniority never let their underlings forget it.

Some addicts thrive on this independent, rigidly structured, closed system. Others find it worse than no program at all. My experience indicates that the social-movement aspect of the program attracts those who very much need some well-defined values and structures. For the remaining addicts Synanon is an anathema.

Recently the growth of Synanon has led to some unexpected acceptance by the larger society. Several facilities, started by people who came from Synanon houses, have been receiving substantial subcontracts and payments for services rendered to individuals. In some cases, this seems to have been their undoing. Outside funding also involves being accountable to a board of directors who may at times interfere with the program.

In San Francisco Synanon games are held for private citizens and addicts at virtually no fee. They are well-attended and apparently successful. This is a hopeful development in that it brings the public into the house and allows the residents to meet people who are also in need of help even though they may not be on drugs. This widens and sharpens the perspectives of both groups: for the public, addicts are no longer dope fiends with blood dripping from their fangs; for addicts, they are not the only ones with personal problems.

Synanon has been subjected to pressures and vilified by professionals, sometimes because it has been more successful than they have in working with addicts. At other times it has been looked upon by some professionals as being endowed with a magical talent to help all addicts. The phenomenon of communal living coupled with a highly structured set of working relationships and a well-defined, commonly shared set of mores fills a wide range of needs for all individuals. At a point in history when the family structure is weak, working relationships are often ill-defined, and older systems of moral and religious values are being challenged, Synanon would represent a safe harbor for many people, not only those addicted to drugs or alcohol.

It must be stated that the original idea was good, that some houses may still function in that same way, but that others have been used by hustlers who took advantage of residents for their own ends. Whether it is due to lack of space, too much notoriety and success, or just plain avarice, according to some reports some houses now charge residents high fees and others demand the surrender of any personal property on arrival. In some cases, such as in Westport, Connecticut, houses have been closed; some others remain open only through sustained efforts. The force of public opinion against such houses has contributed to closings.

The closed society of the Synanon house has been partially opened, at least in San Francisco. This development may be the harbinger of bigger and better things. A social movement reaches a point when it makes itself socially relevant and accessible or it disappears. However, dangers are involved in opening the doors: a reduction in the impact of social insulation and the danger of various kinds of operators taking advantage of the Synanon tradition without taking part in the work necessary to establish and maintain that tradition.

Synanon was the first to focus public attention on the addict and the possibility of his leading a drug-free life. It was not the first program; there were many pioneers in the United States Public Health Service and other settings. But it was the first self-sustaining effort which held the promise of a new life for formerly addicted people. The people who started it and the people who now sustain it should be remembered for this positive contribution.

The lesson inherent for the larger society in the Synanon tradition is that we don't always know what is best, "we" meaning professionals, agencies, legislators, and society at large, and "best" meaning the most effective kind of program to deal with any given problem.

The beginning use of the nonprofessional or subprofessional or paraprofessional therapist in dealing with human problems is now fairly well-established. The realities of manpower problems, the complexities of the problems which face us, and the naiveté of most middle-class professionals concerning the mores and customs of the ghetto all point toward the establishment and maintenance of a partnership of a skilled professional and a skilled nonprofessional therapist. Through their joint efforts they can accomplish more than either working alone. And this type of partnership would obviously extend far beyond the drug problem as an isolated phenomenon into other programs which deal with areas like alcoholism and poverty programs.

It seems clear now that group process is the key to all effective programs. Basically a peer-group process of resocialization that is effective in changing dishonest and immature behavior compensates for earlier groups, including the family, which were not effective in socializing the potential addict. The group process has thus become the major component of private self-help groups (such as Synanon, Daytop, and Renaissance), as well as of tax-supported programs.

The self-help programs seem to be most effective with

the middle-class addicts who at some point in their lives believed in the accepted social values. Their guilt at having broken with these values seems to be the primary pressure point for peer-group influence in resocialization. For the ghetto addict drug addiction is much more socially acceptable (or at least less a cause for social ostracism), and other kinds of influences seem to change his behavior patterns. Methadone maintenance combined with group process seems to be more appropriate for the ghetto addict. The current use of various forms of therapeutic treatment in a comprehensive program, with each addict receiving help based upon what works for him, would seem to be the best overall approach. The considerations mentioned here are obviously only a part of the picture.

15 : SOME DEEPER MEANINGS

There are several levels of observation when one attempts to synthesize from experience and convey this synthesis to others. The scientist sees commonality and patterns and behavior; the anthropologist sees cultural effects; the reporter sees a series of related events; the historian searches for roots in the past. Finally we try to put everything together. A search for meaning is more than a professional pursuit—in relation to drug addiction or anything else. And the search for meaning may be the link that ties us all together.

Two generations ago people were largely occupied with survival and all that this entails, in a largely rural and small-town nation. Our parents witnessed major social upheavals, with the Depression and two world wars. The present generation of young adults represents those caught in the middle of several conflicting forces—the urbanization of our nation and the dawn of the space age, which followed on the heels of the computer revolution and led to an age of plastic-laminated artificiality in which the lines are being blurred between natural and man-made, mind and body, and persons and things. Both the older symbiosis of man and animal and animals (including man) and their natural settings are being radically altered. The entire collage of current human experience induces a sense of unreality by its very quality of unnaturalness. The personal qualities of being human and real and relevant are not currently in vogue. Everything seems to be a big put-on, a farcical, nonsensical joke. And the laughter is hollow, for the joke is on all of us.

With an artificial world comes plastic experience, joy in a bottle, happiness in a lump of sugar, and relief in a capsule. When the world comes back again, too much of it and too soon, oblivion through a needle sometimes can seem like the only answer. It is not an answer. It does relieve one somewhat. There are times when a person is in a corner, and he thinks he'll just try it this once. He just needs a little rest; then things will begin to get better. They have to get better, because how could they possibly get worse? But then they do. And he goes back for more. And more. And more. And one day it dawns upon him . . . he is too far in to get out without a hand to hold on to. And so very few hands are extended, for the pain of others may be even greater than his. Or maybe they don't really give a damn, or maybe they don't understand. But by this time, the excuses of others don't seem very important . . . the only sense of himself available to him is one of being alone, cut off, and in pain. And this is perhaps the story of many of us, addicts or not.

But this is not new, for such feelings are inherent in the human condition. Not many years ago it was common knowledge among common folk that one does not whimper when faced with such harsh realities. But then people had some sense of how they fitted into the scheme of things; there were quiet places and quiet times built into their lives. This has changed, and the change hurts. There is no time to think, to be with oneself, to attempt to lay straight again the scattered sticks of one's life.

Scheming is a hollow substitute for having a sense of where one fits into the pattern of things. As creatures, we have come to depend upon our creation of artificial patterns rather than trusting our ability to recognize the patterns which exist separate from our clumsy meddling. Thomas Jefferson once admonished us to "take things by the smooth handle." But the handles have disappeared. We are left with muscles we never use, efforts left unexpended, and a kind of sense of obsolescence and disconnected irrelevancy.

A city is not a natural phenomenon. It is the bastard child of commerce, born of necessity, with people stacked on top of one another, struggling against nearly impossible odds. For most city residents, under present conditions, the city induces fear, suspicion of the motives of others, and alienation from themselves and everyone else. Chronic anxiety walks the streets. The city is not a natural setting, and yet the population of our cities is increasing each year.

Are we then giving up and admitting that we desire the artificial over the natural? Not really, for agricultural monopolies and technological innovation have made the skilled and the unskilled gravitate to commercial centers for economic survival. The skilled and the unskilled, white, black, and other shades . . . from the South and the Midwest . . . are being uprooted, and like a nation of Okies, heading for the cities.

And when we get there, what do we give up for what we gain? It takes a generation or two or three (depending on a number of factors) to gain acceptance in the larger society. Meanwhile the children of immigrants are left to their own devices, not always through neglect, but through necessity. The struggle for survival in the city takes a merciless toll of the unprepared.

So where do we go from here? The problems are broad and extremely complex. Given time and good faith, all things are possible. We don't have a lot of time left to begin to deal with the problems, but good faith seems to be rising among many people. When this has happened in the past, when people became very concerned and very involved, then problems came into focus. Without concern and the broad-range community involvement of many people, the most valiant efforts from a few will have little or no effect.

Workers in various fields of human services have labored long and hard for many years to sustain life and provide education and jobs. But they are getting tired, and they need help. And unless help is given, we will all pay dearly in the future for our apathy. Problems of national dimensions require national attention and national effort. The nation begins with you and me. Then there are your neighbors, and the people you work with, and the people in trouble. Should you help? Is it really any of your business? Why don't you ask if there is something you can do? Maybe you can help, there or somewhere else. For it is certain that your help is needed somewhere, even if it is only for one hour a day.

Perhaps we should all ponder what it will mean if we *don't* make an effort toward commitment. You are involved by virtue of being here. Whether or not you do something over and above what you are doing will have to be left to you, but be aware of this—what we don't do may be our epitaph!

Involving everyone has implicit dangers; it can be overly exclusive or overly inclusive. By saying the entire community must be involved in the drug-problem-solving process, one may err in the direction of saying, in effect, that no one person needs to take leadership. This, of course, is absurd. We shall need community, political, business, industrial, labor, professional, ex-addict, human-services, and agency leaders, as well as ordinary citizens both young and old. In consort they will find some solution in light of the extent of the local problem and the local resources. The young should be included at the policy-making level. They know the problems and know what is likely to work.

Action is required. A committee "to study the problem and recommend solutions" won't do it. The blue-ribbon committee, by virtue of being blue ribbon, would take a year to educate and another year to reach viable alternatives, most of which could be successfully ignored by governmental bodies. An action-oriented group will admittedly make a few mistakes in judgment, but even if they do something wrong, at least they are doing something rather than merely talking about it. The process may begin with one family or one individual; interest in the problem currently would almost guarantee a response from others. There are many things that can be done: organizing drug hot-lines and drop-in centers, setting up storefront operations for information and referral, and implementing educational programs planned and executed by young people. Most students are bored with the efforts of educators who know little about the problem.

Inclusion of slum-dwellers, exaddicts, and the young will prevent a lack of inertia. Inclusion of other groups will provide whatever amount of know-how in administrative, scientific, and technical areas is needed for sound program development.

And, in this process, different kinds of people may find out that they are basically the same kinds of people, which will provide a solid base for all of us to work from in the future, whatever the problem and whatever the issue. We have somehow evolved as a nation away from the idea of participation in community affairs. This is a concept we must recapture. If we continue to blame the police, or the agencies, or the professionals, or the pushers, or the addicts, or the social conditions, or whatever other scapegoat one might pick, maybe a total attack will never be mounted.

On the other hand, just as the individual is capable of much more than he will ever be able to recognize, groups of such individuals can do even more. For the group collectively can uncover in one another the potential for doing virtually anything. That kind of exciting growth can begin a process for which none of us can imagine the eventual outcome. And regardless of the initial problem involved, people who are turned on to their own potential will not rest until they have seen the quality of life improved for *all* the members of their community.

If there are to be the predicted revolutionary changes in our lives by the year 2000, it behooves us as a nation to regain within ourselves those qualities which will make it possible for everyone to enjoy the benefits. Human dignity, compassion, hard work, and a lack of whimpering will be involved, along with many other qualities we haven't yet discovered or named. We don't have a great deal of choice: Either we begin a revolution within ourselves or we will be taken over by other kinds of revolution.

16 : CONFRONTATION GROUPS

Individual psychotherapy has for years been assumed to be the primary method for treatment of emotional disturbances. But many human problems exist that currently seem to be most responsive to a group setting. The older traditional group therapy has given way to a number of newer group techniques that involve all kinds of people, who may or may not have severe emotional problems. These group techniques have been used extensively with drug addicts (following the model developed by self-help groups). They are effective because they represent peer-group pressure toward attitude and behavior change and because individuals in the age range of addicts are most susceptible to the opinions of their peers.

In the evolution of group techniques many new components have been added during the last decade. All these are combined in confrontation groups. There are also specific kinds of additions which confrontation groups have made to the combination of elements from other traditions, including group-dynamics techniques combined with group-treatment methods. Confronting the addict with behavior that is stupid and immature is the most effective tool for changing his attitudes.

It will be helpful to discuss the various therapeutic forms of treatment by way of describing which elements came from which tradition. First in chronological order is group therapy. A group of individuals who are assumed to be disturbed and a therapist who is assumed to be free from disturbance come together and verbally exchange their concerns and problems. Some feedback (one group member feeding information and impressions back to another) usually comes from group members, but the group therapist is assumed to be in charge. He may challenge, but he also may be challenged. Traditional group therapy has not been very successful with addicts.

Group dynamics and sensitivity training developed group methods by working with a wide variety of people, most of whom were functioning vocationally. One of these methods is the "T-group," or training group. T-groups also tend to maximize the concept of feedback; therefore, they insist on informality in structure and function within the group. T-groups also insist on open and honest communication, whether positive or negative in content, and give much attention to nonverbal cues, such as facial expression and posture, in the communication process. All these components are included in confrontation groups . . . tailored to the addict's tendency to avoid feeling involved.

Encounter groups—a refinement and extension of T-groups—deal largely with an extension of the methods and theories of Dr. Carl Rogers, a psychologist, and his colleagues. Such groups encourage greater leader-participation on the same level as other members and go beyond T-groups, in the sense of orienting the groups toward growth experiences, rather than toward building specific kinds of interpersonal skills to maximize communication among group members.

The work of Fritz Perls (and later William Schutz) in the Gestalt-therapy tradition emphasizes body awareness, total physical participation, and the development of trust in one's self and others in intimate groups.

Meanwhile a number of nonprofessional developments were enlarging group techniques, enhancing their effectiveness with addicts and eventually enlarging the tradition of group dynamics. Confrontation methods are now quite commonly used with addicts and nonaddicts.

Synanon began some years ago to develop a confrontation technique that involved challenging the stupidities and excuses that group members used to avoid the acceptance of responsibilities and their own growth and maturation in an emotional sense. Synanon groups can be brutal at times and gentle at other times, depending upon what the group feels is required.

Within this context of progress in group dynamics a particular blend of components for confrontation groups evolved. They may be led by a professional, or a trained exaddict, or by a person who has been a successful group participant in the past. The groups begin with one assumption—that we all go through a series of maneuvers to avoid confronting each other with what we really feel. A concerted effort is made to deal with the present: what is happening in the group? Who feels what about whom? The why may or may not turn out to be relevant.

If there is a specified goal in such groups, it is the attempt to remove all barriers to honest communication in order to allow for the authentic experiencing of feelings and their subsequent expression. There are many such barriers to being honest in most addicts. Participants may or may not have other serious problems, and they may or may not participate verbally, depending upon their own decision. But blocking the progress by engaging in verbal games is stopped, either by the leader or by another group participant. It is stopped after the process of authentic involvement has taken hold, not by a dogmatic dictum from the leader, but by the desire of the participants to eliminate games. This reflects the degree to which the participants value authenticity in their experiencing of themselves and others. The process is longer and harder in addict groups. Reaching honesty in these groups requires a skillful leader and a great length of time. A marathon session is usually required to break through the addict's defenses. To a large extent, breaking through to honesty is blocked by the nature and extent of the games the participants have run on others or have had run on them. The middle-aged addicts take a little longer to participate—until they become convinced that confrontation is not simply another kind of game. Often younger participants will either never really participate honestly or will try to *make* it into another game and invent their own inappropriate "rules"; for example, they will display "rehearsed" feelings, or try to sound honest, or confront somebody with something in a planned, nonauthentic fashion.

When does real participation take place? When words and feelings come out which ring true and have not been edited by the participant. This is difficult since most addicts are skilled actors. Voice tone, posture, speed of speaking, and a hundred other cues are often used, and an awareness of them can therefore be useful. But more than any other measure for validity of participation is trust in one's own intuitive judgment.

Early in the group, people tend to be tense and tight, sensing a lack of sincerity in and trust between group members. This feels like the frustration of knowing what is not happening and the desire to get to a deeper level. Communication is guarded, and group members are searching. The most cynical addict, however, seems to want very much to reach a deeper level of relating. When the threshold is passed by one group member taking the risk and breaking through the cobwebs, it releases other members to do the same thing. The addict begins to feel more involved with his feelings, more willing to share, and considerably less tense and guarded. It is a process of removing the barriers to real experiencing of oneself and others.

The confrontation of two individuals can be achieved in several ways, depending upon the predisposition of the leader and the degree of sensitivity and maturity of the participant. Sometimes a mirror is enough, for the quiet reflection shows the individual how is he coming through to the other person. The addict is seldom aware of how transparent his "slickness" really is. He can compare what he perceives to what he had intended to transmit. Discrepancies may be ironed out in the group process or digested in private. The mirror requires relatively calm and stable natures in the two individuals involved. Feedback given to an extremely closed and defensive addict is of little benefit —it will simply be denied.

The next degree of confrontation is feedback of a group member's "garbage." This involves one group member confronting another with his inconsistency. The "garbage" may be based on saying one thing and feeling another, lying, or making statements that contradict previous statements or statements that contradict previous behavior. This level of confrontation may be made in conversational tones or by yelling—depending upon the degree to which the confronting group member can control his own feelings at the time. Yelling is required at times, when a person showing duplicity isn't otherwise able to hear it, but most often it tends to close up people who are open to new information. A third degree of confrontation is usually not needed if the leader is skilled enough. It involves verbal attack on an extremely dishonest and extremely well-guarded addict. There are two very obvious difficulties with this approach. Very often it feeds the individual's need to be punished because he is laden with guilt. Secondly, for the real pro at playing games, the attack can be used subsequently, in the group or later, to justify almost any kind of retaliatory behavior. Retaliation is a strong element in the personality of the addict. It is reinforced both in the streets and in prison, which most addicts experience at one time or another during their addiction. Retaliation may take the form of extreme cruelty to other members in the group or of a reversion to older self-destructive and maladaptive behaviors. Even though a group participant may set up himself or his attacker, the net result is a confirmation of his basic self-fulfilling prophecy, that people are no good, and they are all out to do you in if you give them the slightest chance.

Since the basic purpose of the confrontation group is to allow the group participants freedom to practice behaviors other than game-playing, any kind of game must be discouraged. People can and do play various games with one another, but it is also possible that being honestly free of games will add to our behavioral repertoire. When an atmosphere in which we need a particular behavior develops later, the skill and courage may be there. The addict plays games so routinely that being made aware of games is helpful in and of itself.

In developing trust in ourselves and in others, we are usually speaking of the development of an inherent capacity. The person who can trust nobody is handicapped, but so is the adult who feels he *has* to trust everyone *all* the time. The former is rigid suspicion, the latter naiveté. When an addict is able to be honest with others and to build some trust in himself, it does two things. It develops a sense of being personally trustworthy, which is the prerequisite for trusting others. Secondly, it develops an awareness of the cues associated with authentic communication. If an addict has moved in the drug culture for a long period, there has been little experience with cues for authentic communication.

Very little has been discussed in terms of content of the sessions and alternative techniques and strategies which may be employed by group leaders. My own feeling about content is that it is largely irrelevant, since what you say is much less an issue than how you say it or what you do in and out of the group setting. Words are used more often as a screen to hide behind than as a mode of communication. And, most often, techniques and strategies are games that leaders resort to when they feel that something should be happening, that nothing *is* happening, and that they have the ability and responsibility to *make* something happen even though it may be slightly artificial. These games are usually errors in judgment, the result of a lack of confidence in other group members and an unrealistic self-appraisal of the capacities of the group leader.

If you bring together a group of people and tell them what is expected—attempting to develop honest communication, being more aware of one's self and others, and trying to obtain the expression of authentic feeling states—then for the most part the group will run itself. There are times when intervention is appropriate, but in the absence of the leader the leadership function will be taken up by another group member. When an inexperienced or unskilled leader is in the group, an individual with more intuitive skill often takes up the leadership. The leadership capacity of group members is the basic reason why leaders need not be professionals. Other than an interest in people and the ability to care, the group leader only needs to know the sound of honesty and dishonesty and to have a specific ability to ignore words at times in order to listen for meaning and feelings.

In this regard, the best leader for any group is one who knows the language pattern well enough to ignore it, whether this pattern has to do with geography, race, income, or education. The best group leader would be an individual who knew many levels and styles of verbal interaction and who could move in and out of all of them with facility, yet without losing his own particular style, whatever form that may take.

Human communication may be extremely simple or unbelievably complex, depending upon the intent of the message sender and the number of barriers in the receiver. The process of confrontation involves making senders aware of their intent and showing receivers how they can remove barriers to reception. The basic intent, then, is to provide skills in human communication. The basic intent is *not* to cure sickness or to change the basic structure of the personality of the participant.

First of all, Thomas Szacz expressed grave doubts about calling behavioral aberrations a sickness (*The Myth of Mental Illiness,* Harper & Row, New York, 1961). Secondly, evidence to suggest that verbal therapy alone may have little effect on such aberration has been presented by Hans Eyesenck (*Handbook of Abnormal Psychology,* Basic Books, New York, 1961). As Eyesenck points out, most studies of psychotherapy do not account for people who improve without therapy. Thirdly, the assumption that one has the right and the ability to change basic personality structure may be extremely presumptuous. It may be possible to change a person in the direction of your own set of values, but how can you be so sure your values are best for him, or even for you?

On the other hand, there is very little potential danger in providing alternatives for behavior, helping to build up good communication skills, and giving your own views as to behavioral contingencies; that is, what kind of behavior is likely to result in what kind of outcome. Such an orientation provides the addict with a wider perspective but does not require any public admissions of "sickness." In this framework, confrontation group experiences become basically a process of education rather than of continuing the medical model of human interaction. The medical model of diagnosis, treatment, cure is not wrong for medical problems, but in improving the skills of relating, it is inappropriately used. Since the addict lacks responsibility, labeling him as "sick" gives him another reason not to be responsible.

Confrontation groups are necessary because our culture has evolved in such a fashion that honest communication is very seldom used. Social sanctions seem to reward superficial communications between people. Such groups work because there is an inherent kind of relief and joy involved in being understood. They spill over into other areas of our lives because of the rewards inherent there, and the good effects of such groups last as long as the individual has the courage to continue to communicate openly and to live with the consequences of that kind of behavior.

But the risks should be made clear at the outset. When you are honest, there will be those who will disagree and even some who may hate you for it. It may result in a much closer family structure and much more trust among family members. It may lead to a more successful marriage, or it may lead to divorce. It may help you reach a friend, a relative, or a child; or it may drive them further away. It may result in many other kinds of positive or negative outcomes, for these depend upon many factors in other people. But the single constant factor is what happens inside of you—the clean feeling of freedom which comes from removing barriers and ceasing to lie to yourself and others, the sense of health and strength and courage you were previously blind to, and finally the familiar feeling of rejoining the human family.

17 : MARATHON SESSIONS

After the initial introduction of addicts to former drug addicts in a residential setting, marathon sessions are very quickly begun. These sessions helped the largest number of the residents make the most out of the relatively short period of time over weekends. Initially practical reasons indicated the choice of marathon sessions. There turned out to be many more clinical reasons for their effectiveness. Drug addicts have very little trust, and marathon sessions tend to encourage the growth of trust rapidly. Beyond this, the sessions seemed to fit the subculture kind of functioning very well; that is, the group could choose to share or not. Group pressure can be applied to open people up as well as to close them up, and the extended time period seemed to eventually encourage the opening of the group.

The pioneering work in holding group sessions over extended periods of time has been done by Fritz Perls and others over the past five years. Sessions lasting twenty-four hours or more (up to seventy-two hours) with no break are a recent development in the history of group dynamics. There is a satiation, a fatigue element, built into these sessions which elicits material from people that surprises them at times. But in a second stage of their development they find that it doesn't particularly surprise other people, in that most of what was considered by the participant to be a deep, dark secret is common to the experience of many other group members.

The material elicited in the first level of involvement includes feelings of inadequacy, loneliness, and alienation from those supposedly close. Given time and trust, deeply ambivalent feelings toward a parent or spouse come out, along with previous homosexual feelings or experiences, an increasing lack of sexual desire, and a growing slowly away from other people—all these are relatively common experiences. But our stupid customs have prevented ordinary concerns from being shared with ordinary people, so we have to invent ways and means for these experiences to be possible again.

There is much nervous laughter at the beginning of such sessions from those who fear the vulnerability of exposure. There are a number of relevant warm-up exercises, in which a great deal of testing and desensitization take place, and if the leader is able to sit and watch, selectively interspersing some quiet reminders, the ultimate outcome will probably be more beneficial and more lasting. There is a basic human need involved in the unwillingness to be pushed—into anything. The manipulative nature of the addict tends to produce an extreme suspiciousness, and each new group marathon seemed to produce new ways to test the new "shrink" (myself) and to find out what my "angle" was.

Having coffee and food available is a good idea, as is making the participants as physically comfortable as possible. Casual, unsexy clothing will enhance comfort and reduce distractions in sexually integrated groups. Sexuality may very well become an issue, but casual dress will allow it to come up naturally, rather than as a result of calling someone on his or her seductive game.

Marathon sessions seem to be more than just prolonged group sessions. The marathon method may begin with a therapeutic bias (or orientation, if you prefer that term), a T-group bias, or an encounter–confrontation bias. But regardless of the initial set of assumptions in the leader or in the participants, the phenomena inherent in extended sessions take on qualities separate from the initial assumptions held. These phenomena provide the basis for this chapter.

The initial anxiety already described tends to be dissipated—first through the passage of time, and second, through interaction of the formerly addicted participants as trust is built up. But the reduction of anxiety and the growth of real participation are distinctly different processes. In the best marathon experiences the reduction of anxiety is the first step toward the development of trust and the subsequent promotion of personal revelation, but the latter does not automatically follow from the former. It is possible for anxiety to disappear entirely and for no real participation to follow. For commitment to taking the risk involved in personal revelation, and therefore vulnerability, is a very different process from gaining comfort.

The probability of personal revelation of present-feeling states is increased by the skill level of the leader and/or the amount of personal courage of the participants. There is also a tendency among addict groups for an initial prohibition against real participation. A group made up of incarcerated addicts who have had past and will have continuing personal contacts, and therefore probably a number of hidden agendas, requires a great deal more trust and courage from the participants and a higher skill level from the leader.

Fatigue becomes an issue after six or eight hours of continuous interaction. It introduces a new dimension, which begins to show effects slowly and reaches a peak some time later. The effect is similar to a drug or alcohol, which reduces inhibitory mechanisms in participants who allow or want that to happen. There are people wound up so tight that no amount of fatigue will unwind them, and those with a moderate amount of chronic lethargy will simply go to sleep. But assuming that there is real participation as perceived by group members, it is then possible for such a group to continue for long periods of time.

There seems to be a built-in mechanism in the marathon group process which tells everyone when he reaches the peak of full participation, when he begins to unwind—and then it is over. This would suggest that group leaders need not be overly concerned about the precise number of hours that will be involved, unless there are other considerations. If thirty-six hours, or forty-eight hours are the restrictions (such as a weekend session), and participants have an idea of what the time period is, they will usually get their goals accomplished in the time set aside for the session. The addicts nearly always finished their work in our sessions.

Preparation of participants is a vital factor in the quality of the marathon experience. This may be accomplished verbally at the beginning of the groups, or some written material can be prepared in advance. The most important factors to be emphasized are the expected length of the session, the quality of interaction that may be expected, and the way such groups tend to change over a period of time. Such preparation is particularly important for a new group in a noninstitutional setting.

As to the potential leader for such a group, the normal requirements mentioned previously for a group leader are needed, in addition to some physical stamina. If one group leader is not able to function through the entire session, two or more leaders may be needed. Eventually former addict residents were trained to run groups.

The confrontation emphasis seems to prevail early in the group session, with aggressive, hostile feelings quickly coming out. In the absence of strong group members, the group leader may bear the brunt of many such feelings. If this particular process is handled openly and honestly by the group leader, the other stages of personal sharing and any possible affectionate feelings will eventually prevail. The hostility in groups of institutionalized addicts is nearly always present initially.

If there is a large number of extremely hostile group members or if the attack phase of the evolution of the group is poorly handled, it is possible for the group to remain in that stage for an extended period. In this instance some personal sharing on the part of the leader can shake the group out of that stage and into a different phase.

A wide variety of adjunct strategies, such as psychodrama, body awareness, and many others, can be introduced into this group process as well as into any other. Their appropriateness is very often a function of the proclivities of the leader and the flexibility of group members. Attempting one of these alternatives at any given point in the group will very quickly give the leader a sense of whether the group sees it as an addition or an interference. Addicts seldom hesitate in giving their opinions of group techniques.

The original theoretical orientation of the group leader may or may not have a significant impact on the natural development of the group. A characteristic "shaking loose" takes place when the group has settled into a particular pattern, during which an obvious conscious effort to minimize the control of the leader is made by the group as they gain a sense of group cohesion. If the leader is able to be comfortable with this reduced amount of influence, many potential gains can accrue to individual group members. If the leader insists on maintaining primary influence, then the dependency inherent may, in that case, reduce potential benefits for group members—even though it may maintain the comfort of the group leader. The addicts seem to be able to make compromises on most issues except control.

Marathon sessions are potentially a very helpful kind of arrangement for beginning a growth process. These groups are especially effective with addicts. In the best groups a great wealth of personal material is brought out which can form the base for further personal exploration and growth, assuming that continued effort is sustained. A sense of family can develop—a heightened awareness of the nonverbal behavioral cues in self- and other-awareness and a reduction in the alienation which results from feeling that our personal problems are shared by others. In short, it can be a very human experience. As mentioned previously, marathon sessions are extremely helpful in allowing addicts to develop trust, to set aside attempts to manipulate others, and to develop a new level of relating.

18: TRAINING ADDICT COUNSELORS

Dr. Margaret Rioch, at the National Institute of Mental Health, did a pioneering experiment several years ago, training some carefully screened housewives as mental-health counselors. Her study was initially not widely accepted by mental-health professionals. They felt that only long years of schooling, with carefully supervised internship experience, could develop helping professionals. Her evidence was impressive, and she received hundreds of requests from the greater Washington, D. C., area for similarly trained professionals. Recent trends in education, antipoverty, and similar human-services professions have indicated the effectiveness of having trained individuals from similar backgrounds working on a peer level with those who are representatives of the people receiving the services.

Exaddicts are particularly well-suited to function as group leaders in confrontation marathons or on a one-to-one level with other addicts. They have a base of experience in the drug world which is excellent preparation for relating to other addicts on an accurately empathetic basis. ("Yes, I know what it feels like. I've done it.")

Selection criteria would be the same as with any other training program for group leaders—the best participants make the best leaders. Their job requires perceptive intelligence, an ability to relate honestly, and a genuine interest in other people and their feelings. Most of the addicts among the more than one hundred trained during the past year or so have had these qualities. Some of them have been better counselors or therapists than many of the best mental-health professionals.

The training took place at the Mid-Hudson Rehabilitation Center in Beacon, New York. Initially the training was a combination of lectures, reading assignments, and supervised experience in running groups. In other words the traditional academic approach was used. It became clear relatively soon that the lectures and reading were largely superfluous for most of the counselors, and more attention was paid to using problems brought from marathon sessions into supervision meetings as teaching material.

Since the beginning of the New York State program itself has been so recent, there was very little turnover in counselors during the initial period (in 1967 and 1968). Some had been functioning as resident counselors for nearly a year. Some who had left are still functioning as counselors in other settings. The turnover in residents, and therefore among resident counselors, presently is much more rapid, and there is much less time to train counselors. From the beginning the new counselors were picked by those addicts leaving the institution.

The normal period of training before a new counselor functioned independently was reduced from about eight weeks, at first, to about two weeks presently, assuming that the resident had functioned fairly successfully in several marathons before being named a counselor. For several months, I led resident counselor marathons every fifth week. The other four weeks the marathons were run by resident counselors for residents, with no other staff members present in the room.

There are several recurring problems in the training sessions. The first problem concerns the issue of counselor competence. A very early question in each marathon session is, "What makes you think you can help anybody? Aren't you a junkie just like the rest of us?" The resident counselors' responses are usually defensive until they learn to admit that they *were* basically like the rest, but that they had been selected to help other residents talk about themselves and their problems with some privacy. (Privacy alone becomes a very precious commodity in an institutional setting.) Some less comfortable counselors tried to "out-psych" me. Others never made it to any degree of proficiency and usually dropped out of the sessions on their own.

Another recurring problem was the need felt by many to have an answer ready to any question asked. This question-and-answer game can only be broken when the counselor reverses the process by asking the questioner, or the group in general, for reactions to the issue involved. The direct question demanding an answer can very often be a game to avoid personal involvement and revealing feelings. This was only one of the several games used as ploys and gambits by the participants. Many groups began as intellectual chess games, with people feeling out the interpersonal dimensions of the room and the people in it.

One game is called "Man, is this a lousy program!" Another is "You think you had a habit!!!" Another is "There's this chick I got up-tight, see?" There are several variations of all these games, but the need they fill is a valid one during the initial meeting of a new group. After that time, they represent digressions or conscious avoidance and are usually pointed out by the counselor before they really get started.

The learning-by-doing approach was most effective during counselor marathons, in addition to the following-day supervision meetings in which the counselors and I discussed how the groups had progressed. The real participation may be active or passive, depending upon the style and ethnic group of the participants. The white counselors were generally the passive group, the black counselors generally the most active, with the Puerto Rican group in the middle.

It should be mentioned that ethnic lines are usually

more rigidly drawn in institutional or prisonlike settings than in the outside world. To some extent this relieves the anxiety of ethnic-conscious individuals. At the times when the morale of the entire resident population was low, the trouble which broke out was usually based on ethnic loyalties or conflicts. This is the strongest rigidity that is brought into the institution from the streets. Separation along ethnic lines in terms of living space seemed to be condoned by administration during the early stages of the program. It should also be mentioned that if integrated living arrangements had been forced on the residents, it might have led to even more trouble. It is evident that the roots of racism run deeper in all of us than we would care to admit.

The resident counselors generally came to several marathons before they became counselors, so they had a good idea of what to expect in terms of participation. The fact that the residents were in prison had several significant effects on participation. In a facility the program is quite different than one in which addicts are dealt with on an out-patient basis for which features would have to be added. In the institution it is necessary to offer incentives to participation. We offered coffee and an extra pack of cigarettes for the day of the marathon. Some residents came down for these incentives alone—but some of them continued to participate also.

The resident counselors functioned with this set of realistic expectations (i.e., knowing about less than enthusiastic participants). In addition it was emphasized that the marathons were intended to offer residents a new kind of skill in relating, which would begin a new process. But this process would be continued in other ways and in other settings in the institution by staff members and residents.

The participation training during the marathons for the counselors alone were not teaching-oriented, though learning did take place. The atmosphere of the training groups was the same as that intended for other group sessions; that is, personal material not previously shared with others was considered a good place to start.

According to resident counselors, the orientation begun in the training groups was reported to have carried over quite well into resident marathons. The style of participation of a resident counselor in counselor marathons tended also to carry over to resident marathons. It may have been a hard or soft approach, an active or a passive style, but the hallmarks of the more successful counselors were constant, in spite of these individual differences. These were qualities behind the words, which were sensed by other residents—caring, the courage to be real, and the patience to listen carefully.

There are many schools of psychotherapy and many theories of counseling. The more esoteric philosophical bases for the entire process of human growth, such as the recent European imports, include the existential and phenomenological frames of reference. Gestalt therapy (and, many years back, general Gestalt psychology) are also imported. In recent years most schools and theories have been losing their sharp distinctions. Some therapists admit the huge difference between initial training and orientation and their present style of functioning.

In this respect it is difficult to tell what aspect was borrowed from where. Most of the time it doesn't seem to be of major importance. The single criterion for relevance to the New York State program was what works—what is of real help and what isn't. Within the confines of the setting described, the methods described seemed to work the best. Whether or not these methods and procedures (or more precisely which of the many) will work in another setting must be left to the intuitive judgment of the professional involved.

The basic message inherent in this chapter is that former addicts can be trained to function as counselors without much difficulty. They have a set of personal needs and characteristics which prepare them well for this kind of work. And the job satisfaction inherent in helping other people can be sufficient, outside the institution, to keep them away from drugs.

Programs are springing up throughout the country to help addicts. Other than the private programs, very few use exaddict counselors but depend on professionals alone. From my experience this is a basic error. The *peer* relationship—not the "superior" professional condescending some superficial measure of involvement to the "inferior" exaddict—between professional and the trained-exaddict counselor holds great promise for dealing with this very complex problem. With regard to other complex problems, this basic message gets translated: We all have much to learn from one another.

19 : SOCIAL IMPLICATIONS

There once was a dream. It was called the American dream. You take a wide expanse of land, you import people from all over, you give them a measure of freedom, and you turn them loose. Just stand out of their way. They'll be able to *do* anything. The melting pot and the land of opportunity, the last best hope of other failures, of other times and places. It did not fail . . . it has come true . . . we can *do* anything: rockets to the moon, gigantic structures, advances in science and technology. We can do, but what can we be . . . what could we become? Nobody really knows the ultimate potential of man. Sometimes it seems as if we don't really care. You are what you do . . . maybe. But a person is not defined by his job or his behavior at any given moment.

Maybe we need to study human potential carefully. This may sound totally unrelated to the problem of drug addiction and rather pretentious.

Take a social problem—almost any one will do, crime, alcoholism, drug addiction, riots, and so forth. All are defined by the larger society with one voice: "This is a problem; what is wrong with those people?" What is wrong with the people, and what is the problem? That puts it "out there" at a safe distance from us. We know we followed the rules; we made it the hard way. And we haven't been given any of the medals we expected, so it has to be "them" and "us." THAT is the problem. A sense of community requires that we abandon all pronouns except *I* and *we*, and that we abandon all humane efforts which are not defined by how the "I" can make the "we" more real and lasting.

We can do anything as a group, so we can create a community, a city, a state, even a nation oriented toward improving the quality of life for everyone. We can arrange things so that each of us will feel that a part of his work is to make it easier for someone else to realize the best that is in him.

This is not a social prescription, given *ex cathedra* in the solemn tones of a guru. It is what has worked in the past. A strong sense of self leads to a strong sense of extended self—the community. A group of strong communities make up a strong state, and so on.

You have potentials which you are not using. The

potentials for working, for learning, for loving, and for living are all there. But you must be aware of them first; that is perhaps the most difficult part of the entire process. It will take a great deal of struggle to get them out and use them. But then if you are human, you have had experience with struggling. Struggling is living. So why struggle with trivia . . . why not take on something which will validate your struggle rather than making it absurd?

Social implications cover us all. We have problems. This book is about only one problem—drug addiction. But wearing blinders so that the social implications of the drug problem *alone* are discussed is still wearing blinders.

Where did the causes originate? These causes have already been discussed in some detail. Urbanization, industrialization, the economic definition of a man's worth, family disorganization, ghettos, and racism, they all contributed. As a nation where did we make our mistakes in attempting to deal with these problems? In assuming that we could legislate conformity to middle-class morality, in taking the word of people who said they had *the answer* rather than an approach, in refusing to accept personal and community responsibility, and in many other ways we have failed ourselves.

Can we *really* solve this problem? We can do anything, as I have stated before. But first of all, to get the right answers, you have to ask the right questions. If you are looking for problems to work on, you probably won't have to travel more than a few miles at the most. But *working* on human problems is not the same as solving them; you can solve a math or physical science problem. But being human is a problem in itself, so we will have to continue working on human problems as long as we remain human and as long as more and more humans keep coming along.

The part which is in our hands is not so much how we define The Problem, but rather the admission of the existence of problems in all of us and the personal courage to get on with working on them.

We are working, have been working, and shall work on problems. But what we have done is not nearly enough. We have to do much, much more. The degree to which we focus attention on human problems reflects the degree to which we, as a nation, feel that human beings are important. Our current competitive society, based on the rather tenuous foundation of private economic gain, defines human beings only in a functional sense. What can you *do*? What do you *do* for a living? How are you *doing*? My questions are, What *are* you and what can you become? For if you take your computer and add up all the beings who are in the process of becoming, you will have our future as a nation of peoples in your hands. Otherwise you had better just turn the computer off before somebody drops a Molotov cocktail into its cold electronic guts.

20: FUTURE PROSPECTS

If the problem of drug abuse is squarely faced by the community and if effective programs based upon accurate information are designed, the past can be overcome. The comprehensive approach must be substituted for small unrelated stopgap programs. This will require several basic ingredients: education of the public at large, particularly of legislators and the willingness to face every aspect of the drug problem within the social setting from which it has grown. For the problem of drug addiction is so intimately bound up with the entire maze of complex social problems that it is impossible to treat it as an isolated phenomenon. As a nation we seem to be extremely skilled at treating symptoms and never getting to the basic disease and at dealing with results and ignoring basic causes. Poor health, poor living conditions, obsolete educational systems, and generalized social disorganization are as much causes of drug abuse as are any of the possible deep-seated psychic conflicts. A vigorous, broad-based, and innovative attack on social problems would very probably have more impact on the drug epidemic than the present so-called rehabilitative programs, which are conceived after the fact, carried out with some particular kind of program bias, and enforced through legal machinery. The bias may be a medical, psychiatric, psychological, social, educational, vocational, or whatever, depending upon who conceives the program and in what setting it is implemented. Some bias now decides the main thrust of the program and therefore eliminates other components to some degree.

If and when the broad-based social programs are begun, spin-off programs like drug-addict rehabilitation will have somewhat increased effectiveness. The increase in educational and prevention programs should precede, not follow, the building of treatment programs. Until a community can shut off the sources of new potential addicts, treating active addicts is an exercise in futility. Separate from the problem of how long the treated addict will stay away from drugs is the fact that each day an addict spends in a treatment facility brings five or ten new addicts to the drug scene.

Parents and professionals simply don't know enough about drug addiction. Any agency or professional associated with the treatment of addicts can testify that every day all kinds of church groups and civic and youth organizations request speakers who know something about the problem. Oddly enough exaddicts are seldom called upon to fill this function, even though they are best-qualified to speak on the topic. Each governmental unit, from local communities to the federal government, should have carefully selected exaddicts on their staffs for preventive education. They have lived through the problem and know how much is promised by drugs and how little is delivered. In addition, by serving such a function, the exaddict can receive enough of a sense of involvement in community problems for his job satisfaction to eliminate his need for drugs. Involvement in an important and meaningful activity is the most curative treatment method we have at our disposal, and the one most seldom used.

In the future perhaps more than anything else, we need a sense of community. We have problems—in the individual, in the family, and in the society at large. Unless we can admit to our common problems and attack them as a large family would, we shall certainly fail. We shall first have to admit that loneliness and pain are basic ingredients of the human condition, that we were all born into a world that is so drastically changed that we shall have to begin again, that the alienation we feel within ourselves as individuals is the breeding ground for an alienated society.

The rebuilding task ahead is a gigantic one. It will mean that human renewal will have to precede urban renewal. We need to learn to live with ourselves even more than we need a new kind of house to live in.

The addict throws before us a mirror of what our culture has become. Perhaps we reject the addicts because the reflection we see is too sharp and too discomforting, not simply because we reject him as a person. Our preoccupation with financial gain, with youth and personal beauty, with things rather than people—all are involved. The meaning of work has deteriorated to survival and competition. The very old concept of satisfaction in doing a job well has been replaced by bitter competition between laborers, between labor and management, between one ethnic group and another, and so forth. Our technological computer-and-rocket preoccupations have set aside the concepts of human potential and human dignity.

As the poppy is also a flower, the addict is also a person. This lies at the heart of the problem of drug addiction. There are people who use and abuse drugs, and whether this is right or wrong, legal or illegal, is perhaps less relevant than which alternatives we as a nation can provide in the future. We would be wasting precious time to sit and ponder whose fault it is, for there is simply too much to be done and too little time for us do it for such pietistic preoccupations.

Who will do the job? Everyone who senses an interest in our future. No single group is able to solve our common problems, but a little bit of work from everyone can. We need young and old, employers and employees, scientists, professionals, government officials, and people of all descriptions. There will be one job requirement—a commitment to the concept of the potential within us all. For most people the rewards will be great but the wages very little. And the work will be hard. Whatever you can do will be enough to make some contributions to solving the problems we face.

Whom do you contact? Anyone working for the people who need help. The newspaper, TV broadcasts, and the telephone book are all places to find such organizations. Job settings and requirements may vary, but we need your help. Neighborhood organizations in slum areas, poverty programs, institutions and hospitals, schools and public agencies, private agencies and storefront operations, homes for the elderly or the retarded, the disturbed and the addict all need your help.

Prognosticators foresee cities under the sea and computerized instruction and medical care. These are possible, and they are likely to come about. But between the present and the year 2000 the most important revolution will be a human revolution, hopefully a bloodless one. It will involve a reaffirmation that the central position of man is the measure of relevancy for everything else. We must admit that our scientific progress has already been able to contribute synthetic drugs and machines that pace the human heart electronically. We are able to use our computers to play war games or to teach a ghetto child to read. What will be required more than anything else is the reordering of our priorities as a nation. We will have to get out of ourselves and stop whimpering. Things are tough all over, and nobody really has it easy—but we can't find happiness in a bag or a bottle. It is a feeling associated with meaningful activity, and working with people for other people seems to rate very high in this respect.

What does all this have to do with drug addiction? It depends upon your perspective. However, previous attempts to isolate specific problems, such as drug addiction, from their social and cultural context have turned out to be exercises in futility.

The scientist who attempts to isolate any object or event can testify to the difficulty involved. Any service professional who attempts to treat the addict or the alcoholic or the schizophrenic in the limbo of an office or institution will testify to his limitations if he is honest. And the very existence of such laboratories, offices, and institutions allows the citizen to believe that the problem is being solved or the sickness cured or the violation punished. He can, therefore, justify his own lack of involvement. And he can further strengthen his private myth that he is different from "those people" and thus perpetuate the current ineffectual attempts to solve these problems.

In working with a wide variety of human problems it has been my experience that people seldom change their own behavior for negative reasons; that is, because it is illegal or wrong or because one ought not to do that! They also seldom change for positive reasons that have no reality for them; that is, because it's the right thing to do or what one *ought* to do or is what everyone *has* to do. But positive alternatives which are understandable and which provide a new *kind* of satisfaction are very often the turning point, and it lies within our grasp to provide these positive alternatives.

Using existing manpower and volunteers, programs now beginning can be made to work if the members of each community are informed of the problem, the alternative solutions, and of what they *can* accomplish if they do what is required. This will involve the launching of simultaneous attacks on all social problems and will require that everyone stay in touch with what is currently being done and what still remains to be done.

If the people of America were able to build a powerful, rich, and innovative nation, they can surely also solve their human problems; otherwise the other aspects of their greatness will have a hollow meaning for them and for the rest of the world.

GLOSSARY OF TERMS

The following terms include slang which is part of the current drug subculture.

ACID : D-lysergic acid diethylamide, which is one of the first hallucinogenic drugs to be produced in the laboratory.

ACIDHEAD : An individual who frequently uses LSD.

ADDICTION-PRONE PERSON : An individual who is against authority, who is manipulative, and whose personality pattern is one that predisposes him to addiction.

AGITATION : Sometimes a symptom of being under the influence of amphetamines; it may also be associated with the syndromes of withdrawal from the use of alcohol, narcotics, barbiturates, and other drugs.

AMENTIA : The term used to describe a general lack of intellectual development.

AMPULE : A small glass container used for drugs which can be injected.

AMYTAL : Sodium Amytal, which is one of the so-called "truth-serum" drugs.

ANTIAUTHORITARIANISM : A reaction against those who make or enforce rules; that is, authority figures such as teachers, policemen, and parents.

ANTISOCIAL : The description of a pattern of reactions that indicates a total lack of concern for other people, their rights, or their property. As a personality pattern it includes a lack of conscience and aggressive or criminal behavior.

ANXIETY : A set of feelings that includes a pervasive nonobjective fear of unknown source. It is often induced by amphetamines, and it may be reduced by depressants or tranquilizers.

BAG : A small envelope which contains a certain amount of a drug, usually heroin.

BAGMAN : An individual who receives drugs, cuts (adds an adulterant to) them, and puts them into the bags in which they are sold.

BANG : To inject drugs with a needle (syringe).

BARBITURATE : A depressant drug which is especially dangerous when taken in large quantities or when mixed with alcohol. The withdrawal syndrome following excessive use is also dangerous.

BARBS : Any barbiturate drug.

BENNIES : Benzedrine, an amphetamine drug.

BLANKS : Low-strength, poor-quality narcotics.

BLASTED : Under the influence of some kind of drug, which could include a wide variety.

BLUE HEAVENS : Sodium Amytal.

BODY AWARENESS : A technique used to help an individual integrate his emotional feelings and perceptions with those of his body.

BOMBITO : An injection of a mixture of heroin and cocaine.

BOXED : Being in jail or otherwise incarcerated.

BREAD : Money.

BULL : A policeman.

BURNED : Being cheated out of drugs or money or being sold drugs of poor quality.

BUST : An arrest. To get "busted" is to be arrested.

COCAINE : An organic amphetamine which is obtained from coca leaves. It is also known as coke, snow, white stuff, flake.

COP : To buy drugs ("I copped a bag") or to confess to something ("I'll cop to that").

COPOUT : An excuse for rationalizing behavior.

CRASH : Coming down from a drug high.

CUT : To adulterate a drug by adding an inactive substance.

DEALER : Either a wholesaler or retailer of drugs.

DEALER'S HABIT : An addiction so heavy that it necessitates selling drugs to support it.

DECK : A package of small containers filled with drugs.

DELIRIUM : A stage of confusion which often results from the use of drugs or alcohol.

DEMEROL : A drug which acts like morphine. It is often used by addicts who have access to drugs through their work.

DEPRESSANTS : Drugs which slow down the action of the central nervous system.

DEPRESSION : Feeling low or blue. Self-depreciation and hopeless and at times suicidal thoughts are often involved.

DERIVATIVE : A drug derived from a similar but more complex chemical compound; for example, morphine is a derivative of opium.

DEXEDRINE : An amphetamine, like Desoxyn or Dexamyl.

DIG : To "dig" is to listen to, to understand, or to be attracted to someone or something.

DILAUDID : A synthetic opiate drug used as a heroin substitute.

DIURETIC : A drug which induces the loss of body fluids.

DOLLIES : Dolophine, a synthetic narcotic.

DOPE : Heroin.

DOWNERS : Depressant drugs, barbiturates.

DRAG : Something tiresome or boring.

DRUG ABUSE : The excessive and habitual use of drugs.

DRUG DEPENDENCE : "A state arising from repeated administration of a drug on a periodic or continuous basis," as defined by the World Health Organization in 1963.

DYSSOCIAL : The description of a pattern of social behavior very discrepant from that of the larger society.

ENCOUNTER GROUP : An intensive group experience oriented toward personal growth and interpersonal awareness.

EQUANIL : A mild tranquilizer. It is a trade name for memprobamate.

EUPHORIA : Feeling of expansiveness, exhilaration, and extreme happiness.

EXCITATION : An agitated state.

EXPERIMENTER : One who dabbles with a drug but does not become dependent on it.

FEEDBACK : A central concept in T-groups, involving the impressions of group members concerning one member's behavior or personality.

FIX : A shot of heroin.

FUZZ : The police.

GAGE : Marijuana.

GAME : Manipulation of other people for private gain.

GARBAGE : Drugs with a low potency or no drug content at all; dishonest communication.

GOOFBALLS : Barbiturates, or "goofers."

GRASS : Marijuana.

GRAVY : The mixture of heroin and blood which results from back-up into a syringe.

GRIEFO : Marijuana.

HABIT : A habit in drug language means being hooked. It can also mean general drug-taking that is beyond the individual's ability to control.

HABITUATION : The physiological adaptation of the body that follows repeated use of a drug; it involves both drug dependence and drug addiction.

HALLUCINOGEN : A drug or other substance which produces hallucinations; that is, seeing, feeling, and hearing things that are not seen, felt, or heard by others.

HANGUP : A specific problem, for example, "I have a hangup with my parents."

HAPPY PILLS : Amphetamines or antidepressant drugs, the "up" drugs.

HARD STUFF : Narcotic drugs.

HASH : A contraction of hashish, which is popular in the Middle East. It is similar to but stronger than marijuana.

HEAD : One who uses hallucinogenic drugs such as marijuana or LSD.

HEMP : The hemp plant *Cannabis sativa,* a synonym for marijuana.

HEPATITIS : A liver disease often contracted by addicts because of the use of dirty needles and syringes when injecting drugs. It is also known as hep.

HEROIN : An opium derivative, this is the leading illegal narcotic.

HIGH : In drug language, this is a euphoric feeling which results from the use of narcotics, amphetamines, or barbiturates.

HIT : To make a score (successfully steal drugs or money) or inject another person with drugs.

HOOKER : A prostitute.

HORSE : Heroin.

HOT : Stolen goods or a person being sought by narcotics agents, police, or drug dealers.

HOT SHOT : A lethal dose of heroin, usually administered purposely in order to eliminate an addict-informer.

HUSTLER : A drug addict who runs con games; a prostitute or pimp.

HYPNOTIC : A drug inducing a trancelike state.

ICE-CREAM HABIT : The taking of heroin infrequently and in small doses.

JOB : To inject drugs.

JOINT : A marijuana cigarette.

JONES : A habit.

JOY POP : To inject drugs under the skin but not directly into a vein.

JUNK : Heroin.

JUNKIE : Heroin addict.

KICK : Stop using drugs.

KICKING COLD : Stopping use of drugs without medical assistance.

KY : Street term for federal narcotics hospital in Lexington, Kentucky.

LIBRIUM : The trade name for a commonly used tranquilizer.

LOCOWEED : Marijuana.

LSD : A hallucinogen, d-lysergic acid diethylamide which was one of the first to be produced in the laboratory.

MAINLINE : To inject drugs directly into the vein.

MAN : Anyone in authority; for example, a policeman.

MARATHON : A group encounter which takes place over an extended period of time.

MARIJUANA : The stems and leaves of *Cannabis sativa.*

MESCALINE : A natural hallucinogen, which is obtained from the buttons of the mescal cactus.

METHADONE : A synthetic narcotic used in some drug-substitution programs.

MIKES : Micrograms, the measure used for drugs like LSD.

MISS EMMA : Morphine, an opiate drug.

NARCO : Narcotic-squad detective.

NARCOTIC : A drug which induces sleep and relieves pain.

NEMBIES : Nembutal, a barbiturate.

NICKEL BAG : The amount of a drug which can be obtained for five dollars.

NOD : Nearly go to sleep under the influence of heroin.

NOVOCAIN : The trade name for a derivative of cocaine.

OPIATE : A narcotic drug obtained from *Papaver somniferum.*

PAPER : A prescription for drugs.

PARANOIA : Psychotic suspiciousness, the feeling that people are plotting against you.

PAREGORIC : A mild opiatelike drug.

POP : Shoot a drug with a needle or syringe.

POT : Marijuana.

POTENTIATION : The combined effects of two drugs which enhance the resulting feelings.

PREDISPOSITIONAL FACTORS : Those characteristics that predispose one to drug abuse.

PSYCHEDELIC : The description of drugs, such as LSD, which affect the mind.

PSYCHIATRIST : A medical doctor who specializes in the study and treatment of mental illness.

PSYCHODRAMA : A technique in which people take parts in helping the protagonist work through a crisis situation.

PSYCHODYNAMICS : The interrelationship of psychic motivations for behavior.

PSYCHOLOGIST : A person with professional experience in the science of psychology.

PSYCHOPATHIC : The description of personality disorders such as extreme manipulativeness, lack of conscience, and shallow interpersonal relationships.

PSYCHOTHERAPY : A process oriented toward relief of mental disturbances.

PSYCHOTIC : One who is unable to distinguish between reality and illusion.

PUSHER : Dealer in drugs.

RED BIRD : Seconal, a barbiturate which is also known as Red Devil.

REEFER : A marijuana cigarette.

ROACH : The butt of a marijuana cigarette.

ROPE : Marijuana or hemp.

RUN : A specific length of time on a drug.

RUSH : The welling-up of feeling experienced right after a shot of heroin.

SAN FRANCISCO BOMB : A mixture of heroin, cocaine, and LSD.

SCENE : A place or situation.

SEDATIVE : A drug which induces sleep.

SHRINK : Slang term for a psychiatrist or psychotherapist.

SHUCKING : "Comin' through shuckin' " means faking it when you don't know what you're talking about.

SIDE EFFECTS : Indirect effects of drugs, such as memory losses from taking barbiturates.

SKIN POPPING : Injecting a drug under the skin but not directly into a vein.

SMACK : Heroin.

SMOKE : Marijuana.

SNIFFING : Inhaling a drug, also known as snorting.

SNOW : Heroin or cocaine.

SODIUM AMYTAL : A "truth-serum" drug.

SPEED : Methedrine. Also generally used to refer to any amphetamine.

SPEED FREAK : An amphetamine addict or, more specifically, a Methedrine addict.

SPIKE : A syringe used for drug injections.

SQUARE : A "straight" person; one who doesn't use drugs.

STASH : A hidden supply of drugs.

STICK : A marijuana cigarette.

STIMULANT : An amphetamine.

STONED : To be high on drugs.

STP : The put-on name of a new hallucinogen.

STREET STUFF : Drugs of unknown quality and strength.

SWISS PURPLE : High-quality LSD.

TASTE : A small dose of heroin or other drug.

T-GROUP : Sensitivity-training group.

TOLERANCE : The phenomenon of needing more and more of a drug to feel the same effect.

TOXIC : Poisonous.

TRACKS : Scar tissue which is the result of repeated injections.

TRICK : A person who pays for sex, or to prostitute. To turn a trick is to procure.

TRIP : An LSD session.

TURNED ON : High on drugs, aroused.

UNCLE : A federal agent.

UPPERS : Amphetamine drugs.

USER : A person who takes drugs.

WAKE-UPS : Amphetamine drugs.

WASTED : High on drugs; beaten up or killed; or being in a deteriorated state from drugs or alcohol.

WEED : Marijuana.

WEEKEND HABIT : A small habit, usually controlled, for the employed addict.

YELLOW JACKETS : Nembutal, a barbiturate.

LIST OF ADDICTION REFERRAL SERVICES THROUGHOUT THE UNITED STATES

This list is not meant to be comprehensive; it is intended to give the reader a general, basic referral source for locating nearby agencies which are equipped to handle wide-spectrum drug problems. A list of this sort changes constantly, and new agencies are being formed all the time. The reader is advised to write to the National Institute of Mental Health for a complete directory of agencies and up-to-date information on drug problems.

ALABAMA

State Vocational Rehabilitation Service, 621 South 18th, Birmingham

Huntsville Mental Health Clinic, 304 Eustis St., Huntsville

Bryce Hospital, Tuscaloosa

Hill Crest Hospital, 700 5th Ave., S., Birmingham

ALASKA

Langdon Psychiatric Clinic, 207 E. Northern Lights Blvd., Anchorage

ARIZONA

Narcanon, 1441 E. Clarendon, Phoenix

Maricopa County General Hospital, 3435 W. Durango St., Phoenix

Teen Challenge, 21 W. Willetta, Phoenix

CALIFORNIA

East Los Angeles Narcotics Prevention Project, Boyles Heights Center, 507 Echandia St., Los Angeles

Economic and Youth Opportunity Agency, Narcotics Div., 314 W. Sixth St., Los Angeles

Mendocino State Hospital, Box X, Talmage

California Rehabilitation Center, Box 841, Norco

Synanon, 140 Walnut St., San Diego

Synanon, 1351 Pacific Coast Highway, Santa Monica

Narcotic Addiction Outpatient Program, 1102 South Crenshaw Blvd., Los Angeles

Teen Challenge, 2263 South Hobart, Los Angeles

COLORADO

Larimer County Mental Health Clinic, 1020 Doctors Lane, Ft. Collins

E. John Brady Hospital, PO Box 640, Colorado Springs

Colorado State Hospital, 1600 W. 24th St., Pueblo

CONNECTICUT

Department of Mental Health, Alcohol and Drug Dependence Division, Blue Hills Hospital, 51 Coventry St., Hartford

Department of Mental Health, Regional Outpatient Clinics:

50 Ridgefield Ave., Bridgeport
2 Holcomb St., Hartford
412 Orange St., New Haven
Norwich Hospital, Route 12, Box 503, Norwich

322 Main St., Stamford
167 Grove St., Waterbury
Connecticut Mental Health Center, 34 Park St., New Haven
Connecticut Valley State Hospital, Silver St., Middletown
Undercliff State Hospital, Meriden

Division of Vocational Rehabilitation, 122 Washington St. Hartford

DELAWARE

Department of Mental Health, Wilmington Mental Hygiene Clinic, 2055 Limestone Rd., Wilmington

Wilmington Medical Center, Methadone Maintenance Clinic, Wilmington

DISTRICT OF COLUMBIA

Drug Addiction Treatment and Rehabilitation Center, 1825 13th St. NW, Washington

Drug Treatment Program, St. Elizabeth Hospital, 1905 Ward 5, Dix Building, 2700 Nichols Ave. S.E., Washington

FLORIDA

Mental Health Clinic of Duval County, 2627 Riverside Ave., Jacksonville

Catholic Welfare Bureau, Inc., 1325 W. Flagler St., Miami

GEORGIA

Georgian Clinic, 1260 Briarcliff Rd., NE, Atlanta

Bradley Mental Health Center, 2000–16 Ave., Columbus

Park Wood Hospital, Inc., 41 Peachtree Pl., NE, Atlanta

Brawner's Sanitarium, Smyrna

HAWAII

Child and Family Service, 154 N. Kuakini St., Honolulu

ILLINOIS

Illinois Dept. of Mental Health, University of Chicago, Drug Abuse Program, 1604 E. 79 St., Chicago

Teen Challenge, 315 S. Ashland Ave., Chicago

Community Program on Drug Abuse, Chicago

INDIANA

Catholic Family Services, 3857 Broadway, Gary

Southwest Indiana Adult Mental Health Center, 200 Cherry St., Evansville

Marion County General Hospital, 960 Locke St., Indianapolis

KANSAS

Central Kansas Mental Health Center, 676 S. Ninth St., Salina

KENTUCKY

Comprehensive Care Center of Central Kentucky, 201 Mechanic St., Lexington

Green River Comprehensive Care Center, 403 W. 3rd St., Owensboro

Central State Hospital, Louisville

LOUISIANA

Dept. of Psychiatry and Neurology, Tulane University, 1430 Tulane Ave., New Orleans

J. T. Nix Mental Health Clinic, 1407 South Carrollton, New Orleans

MARYLAND

Spring Grove State Hospital, Catonsville

Henry Phipps Drug Abuse Clinic, Johns Hopkins University, 601 N. Broadway, Baltimore

Spring Grove Narcotics Clinic, 227 W. Monument St., Baltimore

Alcohol and Drug Dependency Program, 611 Rockville Pike, Rockville

MASSACHUSETTS

Department of Mental Health, Drug Addiction Rehabilitation Board, 80 Boylston St., Boston

Commonwealth of Massachusetts, Outpatient Clinic, 20 Wittier St., Roxbury

Bridgewater State Hospital, Bridgewater

Boston City Hospital, 818 Harrison Ave., Boston

MICHIGAN

Synanon House, 8344 E. Jefferson Ave., Detroit

Teen Challenge, Box 5992, 4600 Lovett, Detroit

MINNESOTA

Minnesota Dept. of Education, Div. of Vocational Rehabilitation, 1821 University Ave., St. Paul

Mental Health Center, St. Paul Ramsey Hospital, 640 Jackson St., St. Paul

MISSISSIPPI

Mississippi State Hospital, Whitfield

Mississippi State Hospital, Meridian

MISSOURI

Narcotic Service Council (NASCO), 2305 St. Louis Ave., St. Louis

Teen Challenge, Box 4915, St. Louis

Western Missouri Mental Health Center, 600 E. 22nd St., Kansas City

NEBRASKA

Family & Child Service, 2240 Landon Court, Omaha

Hastings State Hospital, Ingleside

NEVADA

Nevada State Hospital

NEW JERSEY

Morris County Aftercare Clinic for Drug Abusers, All Souls Hospital, Morristown

Passaic County Narcotic Aftercare Clinic, 323 Main St., Paterson

Mt. Carmel Guild, Narcotic Rehabilitation Center, 9 South St., Newark

N. J. Regional Drug Abuse Agency, Box 4099, Bergen Sta. Burma Rd., Liberty Park, Jersey City

N. J. Regional Drug Abuse Agency Outpatient Centers:

54 Spruce St., Newark
214 Hawthorne Ave., Newark
507 26th St., Union City

Drug Addiction Rehabilitation Enterprise, Inc. (DARE), 236 6th Ave., Newark

Rehabilitation of Addicted Drug-Users, Inc. (ROAD House), 427 Bloomfield Ave., Newark

Union County Narcotics Clinic, 43 Rahway Ave., Elizabeth

Drug Addiction Aftercare Clinic, Roosevelt Hospital, Middlesex County, Box 151, Metuchen

NEW YORK

State Department of Mental Hygiene

Bronx State Hospital

Buffalo State Hospital, Narcotic Unit, 400 Forest Ave., Buffalo

Central Islip State Hospital, Narcotic Unit, Central Islip

Kings Park State Hospital, Kings Park

Manhattan State Hospital, Drug Addiction Research Unit, Wards Island, New York City

Middletown State Hospital, Box 1453, Middletown

Pilgrim State Hospital, Narcotic Addiction Unit, West Brentwood

Utica State Hospital, 1213 Court St., Utica

Narcotic Addiction Control Commission, 1855 Broadway, New York City

Onandaga Department of Mental Health, Adult Clinic, 423 W. Onandaga St., Syracuse

N. Y. State Division of Vocational Rehabilitation, 225 Park Ave. S., New York City

Addiction Services Agency, 71 Worth St., New York City

Daytop Village, 450 Bayview Ave., Staten Island

Reality House, Inc., 313 W. 145 St., New York City

The Renaissance Project, City Hall, New Rochelle

Exodus House, Inc., 304 E. 103 St., New York City

Teen Challenge, 444 Clinton Ave., Brooklyn

Odyssey House, 309–311 E. 6 St., New York City

Phoenix Houses, 325 W. 85 St., New York City

Methadone Program, Harlem Hosp., 532 Lenox Ave., New York City

Morris Bernstein Institute, 307 Second Ave., New York City

Narcotic Addiction Research Services, Metropolitan Hospital, 97th St. and Second Ave., New York City

Narcotic Addiction Control Commission, Executive Park S., Stuyvesant Plaza, Albany

Phoenix House, Hart Island, 800 Fordham St., Bronx

Phoenix House 85th, 205 W. 85 St., New York City

Phoenix House, Rikers Island, 1414 Hazen St., East Elmhurst

Community Orientation Centers of the Addiction Services Agency:

205 W. 85 St.
160 Eldridge St.
143 Suffolk St.
1720 Lexington Ave.
482 Court St.
579 Hopkinson Ave.

Synanon, 35 Riverside Dr., New York City

NORTH CAROLINA

North Carolina Division of Vocational Rehabilitation, Department of Public Instruction, 305½ W. Martin St., Raleigh

Broughton State Hospital, Morgantown

OHIO

Narcotics Anonymous Group, Harbor Light Center, Salvation Army, 2304 E. 9 St., Cleveland

Lutheran Hospital, 2609 Franklin, Cleveland

OREGON

Alcohol and Drug Abuse Section, Mental Health Div., Board of Control, 309 S.W. Fourth Ave., Portland

Oregon State Hospital, Station A, Salem

Dammasch State Hospital, Wilsonville

PENNSYLVANIA

Addictive Disease Clinic, Harrisburg Hospital Mental Health Center, 203 Market St., Harrisburg

Horizon House, 1823 Pine St., Philadelphia

Temple Community Mental Health Center, 1422 W. Ontario St., Philadelphia

Narcotic Addiction Treatment Program, W. Philadelphia Community Mental Health Center, 34th St. and Currie Ave., Box 8076, Philadelphia

PUERTO RICO

Center for the Investigation of Drug Addiction, Psychiatric Hospital, Rio Piedras

RHODE ISLAND

Mental Hygiene Services, Drug Addiction Clinic, 333 Grotto Ave., Providence

Marathon House, Fish Hill Rd., Coventry

SOUTH CAROLINA

Greenville Area Mental Health Center, Country Office Bldg., Rm. 600, Greenville

Columbus Area Mental Health Center, 2550 Colonial Dr., Columbia

Waverly Sanitarium, Columbia

Pine Lake Sanitarium, Columbia

TENNESSEE

Chattanooga Psychiatric Clinic, 1028 E. Third St., Chattanooga

Gailor Mental Health Clinic, 42 N. Dunlap St., Memphis

TEXAS

Terrell State Hospital

Bexar County Hospital District, Northwest San Antonio Community Mental Health Center, San Antonio

Texas Education Agency, Vocational Rehabilitation Div., 212B Stumberg, Rm. 200, San Antonio

Department of Mental Health and Mental Retardation, Box S. Capitol Station, Austin

Southmore House, 1823 Hewitt, Houston

UTAH

Univ. of Utah Alcoholism Clinic, 50 North Medical Drive, Salt Lake City

VERMONT

Vermont Drug Rehabilitation Commission, Burlington

VIRGINIA

Alexandria Community Mental Health Center, 720 South St., Alexandria

Valley Mental Health Center, 20 W. Market St., Staunton

Richmond Dept. of Mental Health, 500 N. 10 St., Richmond

Roanoke Guidance Center, 1125 First St., SW, Roanoke

INDEX

DR. WESLEY C. WESTMAN has been concerned with the treatment of drug addicts for the past four years. He was first associated with the New York State Narcotic Addiction Control Commission, in Beacon, New York, and is currently working with the Alcoholism and Drug Dependence Division of the Connecticut Department of Mental Health. He also conducts a private practice as a psychotherapist. Dr. Westman received his B.A. from the University of Virginia and his M.S. and Ph.D. from the University of Wisconsin. He lives in Connecticut with his wife and two children, Mark and Charlene.